North Salem Review

Prose and Poetry
Volume I
2011

About the *North Salem Review*

NSR

North Salem Review
Volume I/2011

A project of the Ruth Keeler Memorial Library
276 Titicus Road
North Salem, New York 10560

ISBN: 1451518293
ISBN-13: 9781451518290

The *North Salem Review* is a publishing collaboration of the Ruth Keeler Memorial Library, the Friends of the Ruth Keeler Memorial Library and the North Salem Writers' Workshop.

Future Submissions
Refer to submission guidelines at our website: www.ruthkeelermemoriallibrary.org

Support the *North Salem Review*
The *North Salem Review* is produced through volunteer efforts of friends, neighbors, writers and artists. Donations are appreciated and tax-deductible. Please make checks payable to the Ruth Keeler Memorial Library and note *North Salem Review* in the memo line. We also invite you to volunteer. To learn more about what you can do, email us at: keelerlibrary@yahoo.com.

Cover Photo: Pam Pooley

Ruth Keeler Memorial Library
Photograph © Richard Koser 2010

Contents

Fiction

Non-Fiction

Poetry

Welcome!

Welcome to the first issue of the Ruth Keeler Memorial Library's *North Salem Review!* This journal is an outgrowth of the library's Writers' Workshop and is co-sponsored by the Friends of the Library. Its advisory board is composed of representatives from the library staff, trustees, Friends of the Library, North Salem High School and the Writers' Workshop.

Libraries deal in written words, books. They also serve as community centers and we envision the *Review* as an on-going reflection of the creativity and energy of North Salem, New York. When asked why does one write, Italian author Primo Levi replied, "Because one feels the drive and the need to do so..." Our writers' group has been meeting for two and a half years, helping its members define their ideas and sculpt their words, and this journal is the product.

Many people helped to produce this first issue. The library's trustees gave enthusiastic support, the Friends of the Library acted as co-sponsors, the advisory board provided input and gathered donations, and local citizens and businesses helped us financially. Frank Curtis provided pro bono legal counsel. Suzanne Rossel and Helen Anthony proofread. Phyllis Gargiulo kept track of donations and correspondence. Richard Koser contributed the photograph of the library. Cathleen Sulli designed our logo. Tyler Scherer provided graphic design and Edris Scherer coordinated the advertising layout. Pam Pooley, former library trustee, leader of the Writers' Workshop, is the founder and editor of the *North Salem Review.* It would not have happened without her initiative and drive.

Carolyn Reznick, Library Director

LETTER FROM THE EDITOR

Dear Reader,

This first issue of the *North Salem Review* celebrates the work of our Writers' Workshop and reflects our community's partnership. The North Salem Writers' Workshop welcomes bold, and not so bold, creative souls who wish to read their work, or simply listen and participate in good conversation each month. It's heartening that the Ruth Keeler Memorial Library and its supporters honor space for the art of storytelling, poetry and personal essay. The workshop is a safe haven to share ideas, fears, and even the right word to use. We always see new participants who bring a fresh voice to the table, and who are met by an attentive audience eager to hear more. It's a thoughtful place where commonality flourishes.

We have discovered that writing is a path to meet each other and ourselves. On this path came the energy for this publication. The prose and poetry here was first shared at the Writers' Workshop, evolving from the safety of that circle to you. For future issues, we will accept submissions from the greater community, with the hope of publishing a volume each year. And we invite you to sit in the workshop anytime to share your work.

I am thrilled by the collaboration and commitment of our community. From the library's trustees and director, the Friends of the Library, and kind and generous neighbors such as yourselves, the first edition of the *North Salem Review* is now a reality.

Write on!

Pam Pooley

Fiction

Alice H. Boxer

Traveler

Things changed completely after the body fell from the sky. Tiffany and her mother found it first, on their way to school. It's funny that Mr. Brown and his old boxer next door didn't find it first. That nasty, slobbering dog is almost blind and he takes it for a walk every morning, early. But he said he went the other way that morning to mail a letter. Anyway, I came along pretty much next after Tiffany's mother went in to call 911. Tiffany was on the sidewalk crying in that whiny way she does.

"S'up?" I asked her. She just pointed into the street. There was a bundle of rags. I started walking over to check them out. There's not much traffic on our street, especially that early in the morning. Later on there are delivery trucks and stuff. The delivery trucks are mostly for Momma and me. Well, for Momma anyway. She orders things from QVC all the time. As soon as I started into the street, Tiffany screamed like a jet going off. Eie, eie, eie.

I surely know how a jet sounds. They fly overhead all day long and into the night. Eie, eie, eie. Once a chunk of blue ice fell into Mr. Brown's yard. That time news trucks came on to the street. "Quite a flush." Mr. Brown winked at me while his old dog snuffled around the chunk. I didn't know what he meant until I saw it on the news. Disssgusting!

Anyways, Tiffany screamed at me. "Don't go in the street, don't go. It's a drug man. Amber don't go." I ignored her, as usual. When Tiffany starts screaming, jeesh! Snot starts running out of her nose and she stops making sense. So I walked over to the bundle. It was right in the middle of the intersection at the school crossing. There was a funny smell like raw hamburger. There were no rags. He wore loose clothes and a cover on his head like the shepherds wear in the Christmas pageant. I almost didn't look, but then I saw his face. That's when I knew. Later they said that every bone in his body was broken, but I saw him and there was no blood. I stared for a long time at his face. The eyes were wide open and stared too, but I don't think he saw anything. Then I turned and ran back to the sidewalk where Tiffany was about to fly off the runway. Eie Eie eie.

By then there were a few other kids and their mothers outside. They were mostly new kids, kindergartners and first graders. My mom is the only one on Judson Street who doesn't walk to school. That's 'cause she knows I'll be all right. She tells me that every day when I get home. "I knew you'd be all right." she'll say and then we'll share some Ring Dings or Yodels in front of the TV. Mom watches TV in the afternoons.

Tiffany's mom was out by then and trying to stop the other mothers from walking past the body. I guess she thought they were too young to see the body. It must have been OK for Tiffany and me. She was waving her arms at them and screaming. She sounds like Tiffany, only louder and deeper, like a blue whale. Looks like one, too. Her arms have that blubbery, hangy down thing that flaps when she waves her arms. I ran past her, back to my house. "Amber, Amber why did you go in the street. Amber, Amber ...." Eie, eie eie.

Anyway, when I went into the house, Momma was just getting downstairs. She wasn't sleeping. She gets up with me in the morning and makes sure that I have breakfast before school, just like anybody else's mom. Sometimes she even sits with me and smokes a cigarette while I have a cold Pop Tart or Cocoa Krispies. It's just that in the mornings Momma has things to do. There's the radio and the watching. The radio talks to her. I don't mean like it talks to everybody. Momma listens to all the talk shows like Dr. Laura and that man with the deep voice who makes up funny words like "feminazi" and that man who Momma said put his hand in a candle because of a bad president. I'm not sure if the president made him put his hand in the flame or what. Sometimes when Momma talks it's a little confusing. Once, in the park, I saw a black woman who had a hook and a big bag of yarn. The yarn in the bag was all different colors mixed together in big tangles, but the woman was pulling it and hooking it into a pattern, a blanket for her son in the islands she said. Sometimes talking to Momma is like that. At first it's all a tangle of different colors, some that don't make sense together like orange and lime green. But if you listen long enough it begins to make sense like a blanket. Something to live under. Anyway when the radio talks to Momma first there's this scratching sound. A signal, Momma says. Sometimes that's all there is. But other times there are voices. Sometimes one, and sometimes two. They say things like "Roger, that's a copy." I've heard it, but Momma knows what it really says.

Then there's the watching. In the morning Momma sits in the upstairs window in her room where the radio is. There's a little bench there. She counts all the people that walk by from 7:31 until 8:53. Then she checks it out in her book. It's a green book with Brotherhood of Locomotive Firemen and a circle printed on the cover in black. "It has to be right," she told me. Once it wasn't right and she was in bed for two days. Then she had to order all kinds of things from QVC. That's how I got my crystal necklace and the teddy bears that are dressed like old fashioned ladies with big hats.

So when she was coming downstairs it must have been past 8:53. "Momma, Momma." I wanted to tell her what I'd seen, but instead I started crying, but quiet, not like Tiffany. "Shhhh, Amber," Momma whispered and opened her arms wide for me. "I know, I know. I've been waiting for this. It's OK. It's really OK." When my Mom says she knows, she really does know. It's not just something to say. I wanted to ask her about the things she was saying but I couldn't stop crying for a long time. And then she made me chamomile tea, put me on the couch and said I could watch cartoons. That was a little funny because usually she only lets me do that when I'm sick. I didn't care, though.

After a long time I was getting bored. I could hear Momma in her room, which was funny because it was afternoon. She watches TV in the afternoon. The radio was making those creepy sounds it will do when you try to change the station. "Where are you, where are you whereareyou damnitdamnitdamnit." I looked into her room. The only light was the fading light from the windows and from the radio. I still wanted to tell Momma what I'd seen. "Momma?" "Whatisit, whatisit, whatisit?" "Momma I saw him." "Iknowit, Iknowit." She never turned to look at me, just kept twirling the dial on the radio. She never asked me to explain what I knew.

I went downstairs and made myself a peanut butter and Fluff sandwich on whole wheat bread. It was time for the news, so I turned on the TV. Today was the day for Channel 7. Tiffany's mother was on the news, still screaming. It was about the body. They were saying that the body fell from a plane. Something about getting into the wheels of the plane, like hitchhiking. They said he froze before he fell. As if he were just blue ice. I stopped eating my sandwich and turned the station to QVC. I must have fallen asleep there because the next morning I was on the sofa and QVC was still on. And I still hadn't told Momma what I'd seen.

I went upstairs to find Momma. She was asleep, belly down on her bed, still in her clothes. The radio was squawking and scratching, the regular words weren't coming out. That was the signal it was about to communicate. "Momma, Momma." I tried to wake her up. She wouldn't wake up. But this time there were voices. I heard "tower," and some numbers—"586." I knew it was important. I found the green book and a pencil and wrote down the words in the back. Momma wouldn't mind when I told her how important it was. The scratching stopped and music started playing, real low. I went back downstairs and turned on cartoons. It was Saturday and I watched for a long time. Next thing I knew it was afternoon and all that was on was golf. Momma still wasn't up. I went back up to try to wake her but I didn't have much luck this time either. I was getting worried. Then the radio and the lights flicked on and off real quick. I ran out the front door to get Tiffany's Mom.

The good news was that Momma wasn't dead. But she had to go away someplace. My father tried to explain it to me. They called him after the police and ambulance came. He lives by the ocean with his new wife and their baby boy and never came around much. Momma got real mad once when he brought my little stepbrother around. My stepbrother is OK, kinda cute and all, but they had to go and name him Stanley. Anyway my father said that Momma was sick and had to go to a hospital to get better. So I had to go live with him. It's OK here by the ocean. School is good, there's no one like Tiffany, screaming and crying on the playground over nothing.

Sometimes I look out over the ocean and wonder if the ocean brings things like blue ice or bodies. I never did get to tell anyone about what I saw that day when I went to look at the body in the street. They said he fell from a plane. But I know better. I saw his face and I know it was the face of an angel. Momma always said that she was waiting for an angel to take us away. But he died before he could find us. I think there might be another one someday. So I already asked my father for a radio so I can start listening too.

Diana Richter

Cheers

He wishes she'd keep her voice down. She always seems to be yelling at him about something, and if she'd not holler like a banshee she'd have a better chance of being heard. She wishes he'd listen. He always seems to be so distant when she speaks to him, as though his mind were far away on something else (or as though he didn't really want to hear her).

A "communication problem," their counselor says. Joan, he tells her, speak more gently. More tactfully. Harry really can't take stridency, you know. He's much too sensitive. Harry, pay more attention to Joan. She gets angry, quite understandably, when you tune her out.

So they're off to a start with marriage counseling. They both take notes. They both keep journals. They both practice (or try to) what they're being taught to do, or not to do. They seem to be making progress. They tell this to the counselor. He seems pleased and encourages them to "keep it up, keep it up."

Joan kisses Harry goodnight at 6:45pm on the 18th. She tells him the meeting will probably last long. "So don't wait up," she calls, picking up her keys and heading for the door.

He knows her meeting will last late. She belongs to a garrulous theater group whose members always want the last word.

So he'll be alone tonight with the TV. Alone and lonely.

He eyes the big bottle of Merlot on the kitchen counter. He already had three glasses with dinner. Joan had a couple herself. Good stuff, Merlot. Good label too.

He pours a glass, heads for the living room and switches on the TV. He watches CNN for a while, then switches to Showtime for an old movie. While he's waiting for it to start, he heads for the kitchen and pours another glass of Merlot.

He soon realizes he's seen the movie before, but so what? It's something to do. No stress on the brain. He needs to unwind, he tells himself. He's still getting used to retirement, adjusting to doing occasional repairs around the house, washing the dog, dabbling in volunteer work at the local soup kitchen. He needs to feel good about life, and a little wine helps. A little more than he used to drink when he was working in the city, but not that much, really, he thinks.

His attention wanders back to the movie on the TV screen. She'd say it was a waste of time. Of course. She thinks she's always right and expects her taste to prevail over his. Not tonight, sweetheart. Tonight Harry's watching what he wants to watch. He'll do it in spite of her. He feels his face reddening, his muscles twitching. He heads for the bottle on the kitchen counter.

He goes back to the living room, full glass in hand, and starts watching the movie again. Sure it's stupid, but so what? He can drink and watch and it won't matter, because he's not really following it anymore.

Joan gets home at 11:05. "God, what a lot of talk!" she says, tossing her purse on the couch and sagging into a chair. "I am so tired! I thought you'd be asleep by now."

She looks at Harry. He starts telling her about a movie he saw once in 1958 starring one of the older actors in the movie now on the screen. His eyes are bleary and his speech is slurred.

"Oh my God, you are drunk!" Joan blurts at him. She goes to the kitchen and checks the bottle of Merlot. Empty.

She regards it in disbelief. She picks it up, inverts it over the sink. Two drops trickle out, form small pink puddles. At least he didn't pour water in the bottle to make her think it was half full.

She feels sadness, disappointment. Hadn't he agreed to see the therapist when she asked him please to go? Hadn't he wanted to help their marriage as much as she did? Maybe not, she thinks now. Maybe nothing will help.

They've been in counseling for six weeks, but they've only brushed on Harry's drinking. Other problems in their relationship—her impatience, his not hearing her—are only iceberg tips, she thinks. What's wrong is Harry's boozing, she sees with startling clarity. Is it getting worse, or does it just seem that way on nights like this?

She puts the empty bottle back on the counter and looks at her reflection in the window over the sink. She looks grim, tired. Her hair needs combing but so what. It's bedtime.

She goes back to the living room. He is slouched in the armchair. There is a splotch of red wine on the front of his shirt. His nearly empty glass is perched near the edge of the table next to the chair. She picks it up, takes it to the kitchen, pours its contents down the sink.

"How can you drink like that, Harry?" she demands. She knows her voice is harsh, not the way to deal with the problem. She knows this isn't the time to deal with the problem either. But he only sits and doesn't respond to her, and her concern gives rise to anger. She knows the pattern. So does he.

"What's happening to your liver?" she persists. She's pacing, breathing heavily. "Not to mention your mind. Do you know what it does to you, Harry? How it distorts you? How do you think that affects our marriage?"

"Shut up, you loud-mouthed bitch," he shouts. He lumbers to his feet, stumbles into the coffee table, glares at her as she switches off the TV.

She marches from the room. "I'm going to bed," she proclaims. "Think you can find your way there?"

She bites her lip. Sarcasm never helps, and she knows it. But her anger is making her reckless.

He lunges for his armchair, fumbles for the remote and switches the TV back on.

She slams the door to the bedroom. Goes to bed, tries to sleep. It's midnight when the door opens, he comes in, trips over a chair leg, knocks a lamp to the floor. He reeks of red wine. He must have found more of it somewhere in the house.

He collapses on the bed.

Joan lies perfectly still, barely breathing, suppressing rage, righteousness, self-pity. He starts to snore, loudly,

She sighs, gets out of bed, goes to the guest room. After a long while, she falls asleep. In the morning, she eyes him suspiciously from their bedroom door. He must have a gigantic hangover, she thinks. He must feel remorse. He ought to.

But he says nothing. He avoids eye contact. He dresses quickly, walks the dog, returns to eat breakfast in silence. Later, they sit side by side as he drives their SUV to the counselor's office. They do not speak.

"God," he thinks, "What the hell is wrong with me? She's right. I am killing our marriage with booze. I never used to drink like that—two or three maybe, and she did too, and it was fun. We didn't get soused. At least I don't think we did."

"He's gotten so much worse this past year," she's thinking. "Why is that? Maybe it's my fault. I don't share enough with him. I'm always going to meetings or classes or some damn thing that takes me away, and he watches old movies and drinks. We've got to change our routine or we're going straight to hell."

They both remember the early days of their marriage, the romance that only seemed to blossom after a couple of glasses of wine, the fun they had, the great sex they never have anymore. Their innocent drinking gone awry!

Harry parks in front of the counselor's suburban office. They push open the white door, enter, sit uneasily in the small waiting room. The counselor appears, ushers them into his office. They take their usual seats.

The counselor recaps their last session, asks if the "progress" they discussed then is continuing.

Neither one replies.

Harry clears his throat. Joan re-crosses her legs, twists her wedding ring.

"Who's going to speak first?" the counselor asks, alert to a rift in their "progress."

Harry does. "I got drunk last night," he says. He leans forward, his gaze averted.

Joan sighs.

Harry says he doesn't know why. He just saw the Merlot sitting there, and he wanted it.

"He always does this when I'm out," Joan says accusingly.

The counselor suggests reasons: Harry's boredom, Joan's nagging. Then, helpfully, solutions. He recommends a 12-step program for Harry, a support program for Joan. He suggests that Harry avoid "self-medicating" and urges Joan to curb her impatience and adopt a calmer, detached approach. He is a font of analysis and palliatives, delivered in his kindly, supportive manner.

Joan takes heart. She agrees to abstain from drinking if it will help Harry. He says he'll seriously consider the 12-step program.

The counselor says he's confident their efforts will strengthen their bonds. He urges them to continue their fine "progress" and to alleviate a primary source of worry and aggravation in their lives.

They both smile and thank him, and rise to leave. They shake his hand, feeling encouraged and approved of. They pass through the waiting room, close the door, walk to their car, drive away.

Harry turns to Joan and smiles. She smiles back. They both feel good about their fresh start.

"Want to celebrate?" Harry asks.

Joan hesitates a moment. Then she says, "Sure, why not?"

Harry pulls the SUV into a parking spot in front of a little restaurant. They go in, slip into a booth. They order two glasses of Merlot.

The waiter puts the glasses on the table. Joan and Harry pick them up, clink them together.

"Here's to us," says Harry.

Non-Fiction

Jean Goldsmith

Fallen Angel

My husband was yelling from the living room: "Hey Jean, is this your friend on 'Sixty Minutes?'"

I ran in. Two rough-looking guys were being interviewed. One of them was at least six-six, thick and muscular, Eurasian with a Fu Manchu moustache and beard. He could have been the villain in a James Bond film. Or better, in an early Jackie Chan. 'Cisco!' I said. 'That's Cisco...you're right."

"I remembered your stories," Richard told me. And: "They're putting him away for murder."

When I met Cisco, he was the head of the Oakland Chapter of the Hell's Angels, probably the roughest branch in the country. He was also working as the Head Grip on our lighting crew. This was in a previous life, when I flew out to L.A. every two weeks to shoot commercials for Bullock's Department Store, which dissolved into Macy's in a Federated Stores spending spree decades ago.

Every morning, as we gathered at 6am, Cisco would roar up in his black Cadillac hearse, chrome skull on the front, with four of his boys riding escort on their Harleys. He had a big gold or silver ring on every finger of his hand. "It's a legal set of knucks," he told me.

It is certainly possible that he and the other Angels were selling drugs at the studio. The Angels are known for that and there were jokes about the 'Candy Man' among other crew. It was not something I would have thought about back then, but I do remember speculation and a lot of nose patting behind the back of an actor who would wear out after about ten takes, disappear briefly into his dressing room and come back full of lightning.

But Cisco was very good at his job and he kept all of his boys in line. If I happened to stroll by, headed for craft services or the wardrobe trailer, he would snap: "Button it. Lady present." and all of those scarred, tattooed, black leather and ripped teeshirt remnants from 'Mad Max' would smile and nod like gents at the Easter Parade.

Then there was the time the prop man called in sick. We had a particularly fussy set up that day, hundreds of gold chains I had wanted arranged like an abstract canvas to go with the Museum theme of the spot. Maybe the prop man didn't want to spend hours bent over the black plexi-glass table, arranging them with tweezers so the surface didn't scratch. I didn't really want to do that either, but we didn't have a back-up prop man, so I arranged them for two hours. At the end of the two hours, the client strolled over, took a cursory look and said: "I don't like it."

"What don't you like?" I asked, without even a hint of 'What don't you like, asshole and couldn't you have come over an hour ago and said something?' in my voice.

"I don't know. I just don't like it."

Sometimes this is client speak for "No one lets me call the shots back at the office, but here you have to do as I say, insert villainous laugh." On the other hand, sometimes business types honestly can't express aesthetic opinions. That's not how the MBA mind works.

"Too angular? Too many items?"

He was struggling. "No, I want all the chains. Just try something else."

So I spent another two hours bent over the table, lifting and arranging chains. "Stunning," my producer said. "Love the squares inside the other squares," the director said.

"I don't like it," the client said.

"I need some direction," I said, rubbing my very sore back. "I can't just keep rearranging it...unless you want to authorize overtime."

The magic words! "It's too much like an airport runway," the client said.

At this point, Cisco sort of eased up to me and whispered in my ear: "You want me to take care of him in the parking lot?"

"Not a good idea," I said. "He's writing our paychecks."

He looked very disappointed, but he nodded. He later told me that he would have done this, personally, as a favor to me, but any other time he could get someone else and it would cost me about $200.

Another advantage of having five Hell's Angels on set is that they know damn well that if anything's missing, they're taking the fall. I have never had a set with tighter security. Every one of those hundreds of gold chains made it back to Bullock's, as well as the mink coats and cashmere sweaters.

Cisco didn't always bring the Caddy hearse. One day he showed up on a beautiful black Harley with an amazing dragon painted on it. When I commented on how stunning it was, he said: "Did it myself."

"You're really talented," I told him. "That's fabulous work."

His face lit up. The next day he brought in about twenty photographs of bikes and vans he'd done. They were gorgeous. Several of the vans had landscapes painted on them that were almost photo-realism. "You should work on canvas," I said. "I know a gallery owner..."

He sort of laughed. "I don't think so," he said. "But thanks."

In his circle, I guess being labeled an artist would have been a sign of weakness.

It wasn't until years later, while doing research for a book, that I learned what happened to him. Richard was right; he was put away for murder. He had a black belt. While in prison, he won the national prison boxing and martial arts titles. Cisco was always good at his job.

My parents taught to give everyone the benefit of the doubt. To me, this meant you treat every guy the way you'd like a lady to treat your brother.

Some men take advantage of this. But the Hell's Angel never did. He always treated me the way you'd want a man to treat your sister.

Only in fiction are people consistent.

KATHERINE HARRIS

LIFT TO THE SUN

Through the window, spring sun, sharp as the glare of mica, bleaches a triangle of white on the carnelian couch where I sit with my leg angled across the cushion, curled forward my elbow tucked into the fold of my knee, my attention focuses on the book opened to a Joan Mitchell painting, La Grande Vallee II (Amaryllis), 1983, its image a structured frenzy of bold brushstrokes in cinnabar green, marigold, citrine, vermillion, and with a swathe of pink above a patch of cavernous dark green, it fills the canvas from edge to edge.

At first a dull rumble is barely perceptible above the whine of the cicadas, yet the soft sound grows to a deep droning buzz. Rising from the drunken dark of the amber floorboards is a bumble bee making a drowsy circle at the end of the room, flying into shifts of light and shadow. The bee swoops from window to window not understanding the invisible resistance. It bumps into the spines of books lining the far wall bookcase. It grazes the reflections of framed artwork. The buzzing is rapid and insistent; its vibration palpable. Honeycombed eyes now open and bejeweled after a winter's dark, are sensitive to color, the Earth's movement and the apex of the sun in the sky.

The bumble bee rests a moment on the lampshade in the center of the room, her voice silent when grounded, and I notice her elongated torso with a halo of burgundy around her noble velvet. She must be the queen. Ancient knots in the wood flooring, shrunken and decayed, leave holes to the underworld of the wine-musty cellar. This must be how she arrived.

Aloft once again, she travels in elliptical rings searching the way to her first deep drink of nectar. Her buzzing is so vibrant that I seriously wonder if vibrations provide a type of echolocation.

She comes closer and I hold my hand above my head as a landing plane and tell her she can settle on me and I will help her. She comes closer and circles above my head. I tell her she can rest in my hair and I will bring her outdoors. She descends over my head and settles on my left shoulder. The buzzing stops. I assure her I will bring her outside, not to be frightened. I move smoothly and evenly to the front door, open it and walk out into the honeyed light. The bumble bee is so quiet and still, I fear I have lost her, but she clings to my shoulder. I walk past the twin cypress trees flanking the front entry and she lifts into the face of the sun.

* * *

All summer I rescue bumble bees. Most bees I find when I'm downstairs in the basement and I hear their buzzes sputter and falter. Some are tangled in spider webs. Yet, all yearn for the knotty circle of light.

I cup their downy bodies in my hands close to my chest. Their vibrations flow through my arms as I ascend the stairs to outside. I walk past the roses and the cherry tree to the frothy blossoms of the rhododendron that offer them a long, sweet drink and watch them nuzzle into the heart of the petals.

* * *

Toward the end of the summer the garden blooms in a riot of color—saffron, cream, lavender and tangerine. I walk out past the twin cypress trees, the roses and the weeping cherry tree to the soft sway in a line of whispering scotch pines and ask the universe if I failed in my marriage. A voice from the depths returns a resounding—no—you only failed to recognize yourself sooner.

DESTA LAKEW

THE ROAD TO THE AIRPORT

The road to heaven and hell, it turned out, is one and the same. It all depended upon which direction you were taking it and whether you marched by foot or were being whisked away in a car, in the shadow of dawn on a rainy winter day, your car weighted down by suitcases. The double lane Bole Road weaves from Maskal Square, or as it's been renamed, Revolutionary Square, ending quite unexpectedly at the entrance of the Addis Ababa International Airport.

On this particular day, I had awoken to the pounding of fists against the steel shutters of our bedroom window. It was Belay. He was outside our window and banging against the shutter to wake us up. The night before we had been informed by the shrill call of the messenger over a loudspeaker that all neighborhood youth were to report to the district office at 3:00am.

Belay was a second cousin who had appeared one day at our gate from the countryside. As was customary, my father had welcomed him in and since then he lived with us as a member of the family. My father enrolled him in the local public school right away. "Education is the most important thing in the world," my father would always say. "They can take everything away from you, but they can never take away your knowledge."

I earnestly believed that sometimes it was better not to know. There is something about knowledge that peels away your innocence and leaves you exposed to the raw reality of life. I was ten years old when the revolution in Ethiopia started. I did not know what a revolution was or how it would come to alter my life and that of those I cared most about.

Today, I knew that there was no avoiding the youth meeting. Belay had joined the youth council of the neighborhood. With his participation in the youth council, the scrutiny we were under was magnified. He had become one of the sons and daughters of the revolution. Family bonds replaced by new ties with comrades of the Party, he strutted around the neighborhood with an air of importance. He had found his place and embraced the accompanying power of politics. He watched us these days with increasing disapproval and spewed revolutionary rhetoric and inflammatory remarks at every opportunity.

"You look like a jolly jack," he would say with distaste if he spotted me in sneakers, jeans and an oversized shirt. That meant I was far from where I needed to be at this important junction in the movement—too Americanized. He was everywhere, constantly calling us out to attend meetings. At a time when trust was tenuous and even family members did not dare express their political beliefs to one another, he constantly stoked the embers fear in our hearts and minds. There were too many young people being hauled off to jail, tortured and killed. We could no longer hide behind the fortified stone fence around our compound for we had inadvertently opened the gates and let the revolution into our home.

The evening chill was heavy as my brother and I left the house to make our way to the district offices. We were the eldest children and teenagers. Once in the streets, he wandered over to his friends and I to mine. Soldiers barked orders and we began to walk along the dirt road toward the district office. It was painfully slow as we picked our way across upturned stones and around potholes.

The bleak compound of the district offices was packed with youth. From there, we are shepherded into lines to march together to Bole Road. "Our mother country or death! We will overcome!" The throng of bodies around me push and pull we are a pulsating creature—stretching out over a kilometer on a narrow gravel road.

Dust and rocks stir, move with us, as we trudge through barely lit streets—soldiers flanking us on either side, in front and behind. Like liquid mercury we slowly grew, absorbing smaller groups huddled in silence along the road to the airport. A human mass growing larger, devouring everything in its path, soon growing too wide to fit the road, we walked in the gutters and along side it. On the narrow center meridian of Bole Road stood soldiers dressed in khaki, the color of sand. The road to the airport was filled with youth—tired, hungry and sullen. Around me, eyes like fetid pools glazed over by a film of brown—shuttered, unwavering.

Through the white scarf wrapped over my head and across my mouth, I pray. Catching myself sometimes, when my voice becomes audible, "Please God, get me out of here." Early morning rays slit open the slate skies. Mountains silhouetted against the orange and yellow-white streaks—the crowing cocks shake their flaccid combs and wattles—stretching their necks to the skies hurtling their voices into the dawn. "Kukulu…kukulu….kukulu."

"Revolution or death – we will overcome!" behind me, beside me, above me—voices bellowed.

The heat of thousands of breaths exhaled simultaneously lay over my skin like a fog. I raise my left hand, fists tight above my head – the words, however, remain stuck in my throat. I felt hands grasping mine—it was Firehiwot, my neighbor, her eyes looked deep into mine—the message implicit: be patient, follow orders, open your mouth, and let the words come out. Stay with me. I rubbed the fear and sleep from my eyes. My fingers came away damp.

Have you forsaken us, God?

As the sun rose, we were finally stationed along the main road. We stretched into a line from the entrance of the airport all the way to the entrance of Revolutionary Square. We were finally allowed to sit. We perched along the sides of the road and on the edges of ditches.

I pulled out the little bundle wrapped in an embroidered cotton cloth that Imama, our cook, had pressed into my hands as I left through the gates of my house early this morning. I took out the two chunks of Ethiopian bread that were inside carefully. This would be the only food I'd eat all day. Even so, I knew that I could not eat alone. It was unthinkable. The saying goes that he who eats alone dies alone. I broke off a piece for myself and handed the rest to Firehiwot. It continued down the line until the last person was handed an empty cloth. Angrily he tucked it into his trouser pocket. I knew Imama would ask about the cloth. But what could I do? It didn't seem worth getting into a fight about.

Today I felt as though there were creatures stirring in my belly—I wanted to open my mouth and belch out my anger, sorrow, and tears—like serpents slithering from the black of a mountain cave. Instead, I spit out dust from my mouth before pressing a piece of bread against my tongue. You see lord—I give myself the offering—damn all those priests cloaked in the safety of your sanctity—pious, droning over loud speakers in church yards littered with people, crawling with lepers and beggars, children without clothes—limbless soldiers weeping—"Let God repay you." Their hands reach out, grabbing, watching sorrowful.

"God will deliver you," the chalice is passed from the lips of one to the next. Eager tongues dart across the edge, tasting tartness. "He will save us from this hell on earth."

"Pray—ask for forgiveness—you have sinned—God only gives you what you can handle…" that's what the priest say.

How dare they say that, picking and choosing the mouths into which they deliver little crumbs of bread? I raise my face to God. Dust settles upon my forehead—my eyelids burning. I press the bread onto the roof of my mouth. I feel the little black cumin seeds Imama has baked into the bread. "Deliver us."

The muezzin wails over a loudspeaker from a distant mosque. "*Allahu akbar, Allahu akbar, Allahu akbar, Allahu akbar…*" Somewhere beyond, the throng I am in, men lay prostate on prayer mats—foreheads pressed to the ground, in neat rows. Solemn eyes inclined in devotion. "Allah is great."

As we sat huddled in the ditches along the road, the city began to come to life. It is about 5:00am. People, cars and police activity increase. We wait to learn what this march was called for. "You must go," my father had warned us, "they are looking for any excuse. Do what they tell you."

Oh Daddy, do you really know what they tell the youth? I'm the one who hears what they do. You don't sit huddled in the hot and smelly corrugated tin meeting hall, shielding yourself from dripping condensation above. While waiting for the meetings to start, we sit in groups listening to the whispered conversations of other girls. What of that girl from the next district, Konjit, who was unfortunate enough to have been a beauty that caught the roving eye of the cadre. He preyed on her daily. Strutting before her in his khakis yelling angry words, spit flying out of his mouth unchecked. His scuffed shoes with patched soles slipped noisily on and off his feet revealing soiled socks, reeking with perspiration. He would swagger before her as she whimpered in a frightened mass before him. "I can kill you now—beat you—maim you," he screamed, eyes on fire, veins crisscrossing along the side of his neck. Hating her for the way she made him feel. Stroking the warm steel of the M16 pressed to his side. "I could disfigure you—right now! Is that what you want?" He left her paralyzed in fear—disfigured, corrupted, emotionally warped for the rest of her life.

Then there was the cadre who ordered my friend to sit in a corner against a concrete wall and repeatedly strike the wall with her knuckles. If he felt that she was too soft on herself, he would grasp her fist in his and strike them against the wall over and over—until she finally fell over, clutching her bleeding hands to her chest—her punishment for giggling with another girl. While the scars have faded, I still see her sometimes, unconsciously, rubbing her knuckles with her thumb.

"Raise your voices—we will now begin the revolutionary chants! Who will lead the group?" We all avert our eyes, afraid to be called on. Not knowing what the chants were and afraid that our incompetence would result in punishment.

"Our Mother Country or death! We will overcome!" someone shouts out. We are merely the echoes of this lone voice.

The road to Bole Airport was, in my estimation, one of the nicest stretches of asphalt. Beyond and in between the villas you could see the fields and mountaintops in the distance. It lacked the bustling note of other areas where commerce thrived and peasants lived. It was an "exclusive" neighborhood of mainly well off families, people whose gated homes had well tended gardens, lush with fragrant flowers. You never saw street urchins playing on those roads.

Today, there were thousands of youth lined up along the stretch of the road leading to the newly built Revolutionary Square. Before the revolution that crossroad was called Maskal Square—and was often used for large gatherings during religious holidays. Now it was an amphitheater with rows of stone steps facing a dais across the street where government officials and foreign dignitaries sat under the shade of an awning sipping cold drinks watching throngs of people in the amphitheater across the street during politically inspired events.

Dusty green army vehicles rode up and down the street some with machine guns strapped to the back. Each time the vehicles passed we would crane our necks looking to see what would follow. Perhaps the time was 1:00pm, the sun was directly above us, when we felt the rustle of excitement shooting down the line of people. A motorcade was heading our way. The cadres shouted at us to line up along the road. Several minutes passed. They seemed endless. Finally, we saw the motorcade make its way slowly towards us. Behind the motorcade, in one of the emperors old American cars, were two solitary figures both in military uniform.

The crowd began to move forward unchecked. Soldiers restrained them with their rifles. The diminutive black figure was Mengistu Halemariam, and beside him a huge bearded man towered waving to the crowd. "Who is he?" someone squeezed past me creating a little stir.

Several voices answered, "Fidel Castro."

I stretched my neck to see this figure that I'd heard so much about. He beamed at us, waving his arms—the crowd had begun feverishly chanting, "Our mother country or death. We will overcome!" The year was 1978.

I looked at this gigantic figure that seemed to weigh down the huge American car he was riding. This was the man who gave up his family's plantation and inspired a revolution in Cuba? This was the cause of our current misery? I did not understand the dynamics until that night when I watched the black and white television screen in our home. Television programming started at 6:00pm and ended at midnight. That was the time of one channel where remote controls had no role in the viewing experience. We saw what the government wanted us to see, heard what the government wanted us to hear. That night the screen showed screaming hysterical crowds waving their arms high above their heads freakishly chanting revolutionary mantras. I was in that crowd. The euphoria seemed boundless. The camera would pan over the crowd and then return to the faces of Mengistu and Fidel. Their chests stretched out—bloated with self-importance, feeding off the energy, smiling—waving the queen's wave.

After the motorcade passed, we were organized once again to march towards Revolutionary Square. There, we entered through the stonewalls surrounding the amphitheater and found ourselves scrambling to find a seat near our few friends. The sun pierced through my head. I pressed my hand to the top of my head and could feel the heat between the cornrows.

We waited perhaps another hour and finally saw that people were beginning to enter the shaded dais across the street. We were urged to our feet by the soldiers. The feverish screaming began again. Mengistu and Fidel were seated as were others whom we could not distinguish from our vantage point across the street. Later on I heard that Fidel's brother Raul was there as well. I did not see him. I was hungry and hot and tired. I wished I could go home. I wished Fidel would go home.

The crowd began to cheer. Here was the man who helped Ethiopia win the war against Somalia. This was Fidel Castro, the man who led Ethiopian and Cuban soldiers to the Ogaden and forced Siad Barre to retreat. The cheers were drawn out. The media—rabid dogs—turned their camera upon the crowd. This was evening news in the making. Eventually, the cheering subsided, the long speeches began. We sat in the direct sunlight thinking only of water and shade.

The day was long. Speech upon speech rained down upon us from the tinny speakers surrounding the amphitheater, each orator hit a higher note than the last, reassuring themselves, more than us, that they were in the spirit of the revolution. The language was new to me. So many words and phrases birthed from the passion of the revolution, multiplying like worms crawling out of a heap of fresh cow dung. My fingers made circles in the dirt beneath me—concentric circles spiraling out of control, until they all melded together into one shallow hole. I wished I could crawl into it and disappear. My nails came away packed with red dirt. I examined them and carefully removed the dirt from under the raw edges of my bitten nails. I was hot, but didn't dare remove my sweater, why draw attention?

I looked around to see what others were doing. A young man who lived a few doors away, had begun nodding off to sleep. Within minutes a soldier strode up behind him and struck him on the shoulder with the butt of his rifle. This infraction would not be forgotten. I suddenly pitied him. He lurched forward nearly sprawling on all fours. Without a word, he straightened up and focused his eyes before him. I prayed that the soldier would not remember his insolence, and that he would be able to go home when we were dismissed.

After nearly three hours of the strident speeches, the people in the dais stood and began to file out to waiting cars. The soldiers prodded us to our feet with angry voices. We began to cheer, wave and sing. We lifted our fists to cries of "our mother country or death." I felt dead.

Eventually, under the angry gazes of the soldiers, we stumbled out of the amphitheater and onto the streets, a tired mass of bodies squeezing out of the exits and expanding onto the sidewalks. Firehiwot grabbed my hand and we began to walk briskly towards our neighborhood. "Don't look around," she warned, "just walk quickly." I didn't need to be told twice.

Brenda Maddaluna

Woman's Best Friend

There has always been a dog keeping me company throughout each stage of my life. When I was a young girl spending long summer afternoons lying on a blanket reading under a shade tree, a furry four-legged canine would share the blanket with me. If I went for long walks, bike rides, or fishing in the "crick," I was never alone. My first best friend was Sonny; a Heinz 57 mutt with light yellow coloring and a tiny splash of white on the tip of his tail. He came out of nowhere and took up with me after I began feeding and hugging him. There was always some stray showing up, even though we lived far out on a dirt road in the country, with no neighbors in close proximity and very little traffic passing by.

At one time I had an amazing windfall of three puppies and eight kittens to pet and spoil. Apparently, the word had gotten out that I was a victim of the Elly Mae Clampett syndrome so people dropped off their unwanted "critters" in our vicinity. In that batch of eleven drop-offs, there were three kittens with long silky white fur and brilliant blue eyes. I took a great deal of time and care about "placing" those gorgeous kittens with schoolmates only after a complete background check to make sure the kittens would be appreciated. I eventually found homes for all eleven, but only after my parents insisted I couldn't keep them. I still remember what a joy it was to think they might all get to live with me.

When Sonny disappeared one day, I was frantic, searching for him everywhere. Sonny had one extremely bad habit—he liked to chase the infrequent cars that passed by our home. One of our distant neighbors flew past our place each morning and evening on his way to and from work. I believed for most of my life that the speedy neighbor had struck my dear friend and left him to die somewhere along the road or maybe injured him so badly that he had crawled off in the woods to die. It wasn't until just a few years ago that my Dad finally confessed to accidentally running over Sonny with the tractor. He had been too upset to tell me and break my heart so he had buried the poor fellow somewhere far back in the pasture in an area I wouldn't likely spot if I hiked out there.

I had two subsequent German Shepherds next—the first one a classic silver-grey color with black-tipped ears and then an all black guy who intimidated any would-be visitor. I always had to go out to the car and hold "Killer" while the slightly shaky person practically ran into the house. I never liked the moniker "Killer," but that was the name he had when he was given to me and I didn't think it fair to make him learn a new one. He really wasn't dangerous, but he was a terrific watchdog and no one could get close to me if I didn't wish it. He suffered from arthritis of the hips in his old age as is typical of German Shepherds. After I had moved out to go to college, my brother felt so sorry for Killer due to the painful arthritis, that he took the sweet old crippled boy out behind the barn one day and ended his suffering with one well-placed shot in the back of his head. Jeff knew I couldn't bear to see my old friend in such pain, but neither could I end it myself. It took a great deal of courage and compassion for my brother to do that and he came back up to the house afterward, sobbing in great gasping breaths.

A few more dogs came and went as I tried to keep them a secret from various landlords when I was a single working woman living in apartments. When my husband and I found our first home complete with ten acres of lawn, woods, pasture and a pond, we decided it was the perfect time and place for a puppy. Erika and James were still toddlers and the sight of them together with that fuzzy Golden Retriever puppy in their red wooden wagon was every young mother's dream. There is nothing like a warm, wiggly, plump-bellied ball of soft fur, licking your face with its pink-tongued puppy breath. We named him Sam and he lived with us for many years until one day he disappeared while accompanying Erika and I as we were riding our horses through some thick wooded trails. We heard some other riders in the distance but never actually spotted them, so we felt Sam may have followed them instead, mistaking them for us in the tangled foliage. We hunted for him several days and left "Reward" posters around area businesses, but never had even one lead on his whereabouts.

Later that fall, Anthony brought home yet another even smaller blonde bundle who fit perfectly into a tiny wicker basket with a handle, making it convenient to transport little Gus wherever we went. Gus quickly outgrew that small basket and later moved with us to Puerto Rico and then on to New York. He survived heart worms and a series of sarcomas that required several veterinary interventions before succumbing to a seizure brought on by his arthritis medicine at age 10. Erika was away at college and James in his senior year of high school. I remember how tenderly James carried Gus in his arms when we brought him to the vet. I was home alone when the vet phoned to inform me Gus had died. I removed his bed and feeding dishes before James came home from school. When James looked around and noticed Gus' things were missing, he crumpled onto the floor beside the spot where Gus had slept and cried. I softly closed the door and left him to his grief. Gus was cremated and his ashes were put into a flowered tin, which still resides on a shelf in the barn tack room with his collar and tags hanging on the wall above.

Many months passed before I could bring myself to think about getting another family member. During spring break, Erika brought a friend home from college and along with James, we all went to a kennel near Mahopac that had advertised Golden Retriever puppies for sale. The puppy in the ad had already been taken, but there was a ten week-old female that was still waiting for a home. I was hoping for a younger puppy, but I knew I was "toast" when the young lady at the kennel brought that sweet little girl out of her pen and placed her outside on the ground in our midst.

She was very excited as she growled, pounced, ran, and played with us. Her coat was somewhat more of a reddish cast than the previous males we'd had and her face more slender and defined, giving her a more feminine air. She also had amber-colored baleful eyes and a deep brown wet nose. And ah, yes! She still had that glorious puppy breath. I hastily wrote the check while the paperwork and instructions were compiled, wondering if Anthony would be upset since he wasn't included in the decision. He was somewhat resentful but soon capitulated when he saw that expressive endearing little face. In keeping with the simple one-syllable nomenclature, I decided upon "Meg," short for Nutmeg, the color of her coat. Anthony liked the official name of Meg-a-Byte for the pedigree papers, but it didn't matter to me, since either way, "Meg" it was.

Since Anthony traveled frequently, Erika was back in Vermont and James was involved with all the activities of "Senioritis," I was left to train, feed, love and enjoy my new best friend. I found Meg very easy to teach—everything from toilet training to boundaries. She listened well and never left our property, so I never had to use a shock collar or the lines buried underground marked by little white flags. She was still into chewing and did quite a number on the laundry room walls, where she stayed when she slept or when I had to be away. She quickly adjusted to her big fluffy bed in the garage and learned to jump into the back of the SUV when I wanted to go for a hike in Mountain Lakes.

Meg became overly excited when Erika or James came home, so they learned not to pet Meg too quickly or she would lie on her back and piddle with her tail wildly wagging and spreading the liquid all over the floor. When asked, "Where's your necklace?" she would start grabbing her name tag on her collar between her teeth and shake it around, leaving tooth marks all over the metal heart shape. She also enjoyed biting socked feet and psychotically chasing her tail in both directions, a behavior she still displays whenever loved ones depart. No other dog I have ever known has given me such joy and companionship with such amusing antics and extreme loyalty.

We took Meg down to the pond her first summer to encourage her natural instinct to swim, being a retriever. Gus had never taken to swimming as Sam had before him, so we wanted to make sure Meg's experience with water was positive. Erika actually carried Meg out to the middle of the pond, which is about neck high, and gently urged her to paddle toward me where I was wading in the mucky dark mud along the shore. After a few attempts, Meg was swimming all around the pond, bringing balls and sticks to us, to throw out into the water over and over and over again. The only difficulties we had were in teaching Meg not to swim on top of us, scratching our shoulders with her nails, and not to bite the inflatable hot pink float or the green alligator we were trying to recline upon. She was certainly in her element aquatically and swam in any body of water she spied, no matter what the season.

One winter day we trekked to Mountain Lakes and climbed up the hill at the back entrance, which runs along a rushing stream, before it passes between twin lakes. Both lakes were mostly covered in ice and there was just a thin strip of icy water between two solid pieces of ice in the northern lake. A small flock of ducks flew across the road and landed on the furthermost section of ice just as Meg and I reached the lakes. It was a clear cold sunny morning and as I was enjoying drinking gulps of the very refreshing air and feeling it fill my lungs, Meg sprinted after the clever ducks who watched as I called out to stop their would-be attacker. They let out a few taunting quack-quacks, lifting off just as Meg ran across the ice, too late realizing she was running out of solid footing. Her paws skidded across the remaining ice while her nails made faint scraping noises just before she plunged into the icy water. I couldn't stop laughing as I heard the ducks make what sounded like louder berating quacks aimed at the startled soaking wet dog, looking around as if she were hoping no one noticed. She was actually limited to a tiny strip of water and began swimming toward me between the chunks of ice on either side. Thank goodness she could swim close enough to shore so I could grab her by her collar and haul her out, relieving me of an envisioned alternative in which I would have had to jump into the frigid water to save her.

We went on with our hike, encountering a gentleman and his black lab. The man was shocked to see Meg's wet coat. I was tempted to tell him I had pushed the sopping pup into the water just for fun. As we came back down the final grade nearing the lakes on either side, I just looked at Meg, saying, "Don't even think of jumping back into that water. You're lucky I was here." Upon retrospect, it's quite ludicrous to say that, knowing Meg wouldn't even be there without me. That incident had me looking closer at my friend and beginning to notice how blonde she was becoming.

There were other hysterically amusing behaviors Meg exhibited which further led me to believe she must have been dipping her coat in peroxide. If I ride my bicycle back and forth on the driveway, she chases it while barking and biting the tires simultaneously. Whenever I roll the push mower out to trim the lawn, she starts snarling, snapping, and jumping back and forth at the machine as I repeatedly pull the windup cord, trying to get the thing started. In the evening while resting in her bed by the fire as we relax in the family room, the adolescently funny sound of flatulence "pfffftt!" will escape from Meg's backside. This sound will actually startle her awake, causing Meg to jump up and turn around, not realizing that the noise and ensuing odor came out of her. It frightens her so much that she literally runs out of the room away from the strange thing.

Her endless games of fetch with tennis balls are much like other normal retriever behaviors, but it becomes so annoying I try to "fake her out" by pretending to throw it so she will go looking for it and leave me alone. When she finally figures out I didn't throw it, she comes back and pushes her nose all around me, looking for the dirty slobbery ball. Then I try to throw it when she's not looking so I'll have a few minutes' peace, but she usually finds it before my "few minutes" are up. Even at night when there are no stars or moon for light, she can find the damned ball. When she eventually gets thirsty after running up and down the hill, she will head for the water bowl and drop the ball into it before drinking. Having a soaking wet dripping tennis ball deposited in my lap is not always a thrill, but sharing an ice cold beer with my best friend helps me forget. Meg likes to slurp up beer I pour into her dish.

I really don't mind sharing with Meg; if I'm hungry or thirsty and I share half then I'm only consuming half the calories. After I give Meg her breakfast, she will come around to the patio door and press her nose to the glass, watching me eat my breakfast. I always let her in and give her both ends of my banana. I also give her carrot pieces and apple cores, both of which I've read vets recommend. I stopped feeding her dry carb-filled dog food long ago; now she only gets canned meat twice a day, along with assorted healthy snacks. She is now a perfect weight with unlimited energy, although not perfectly groomed. Meg runs for cover if she sees me with a hose for bathing or a brush for getting hair clots, assorted stick tights or small sections of briar out of her thick coat. I have to hold her down to remove ticks, administer flea preventative or cut the large chunks of matted hair from behind her ears or embedded in her sheep-like hindquarters. I shudder when we encounter other dogs on hikes who are perfectly groomed with their long coats flowing free of tangles, sticks, burrs or insects. I feel they are looking down their mud-free noses at my truly earthy companion.

Erika accidentally discovered something else that makes Meg run for cover. A few New Year's eves ago, she had some friends over to celebrate and they had some of the usual festive favors such as noise makers, silly hats and those paper horns that roll out and curl up as they make a strange tooting sound. Meg was chasing her tail and trying to bite the guests' feet after piddling all over the floor whenever anyone attempted to pet her, so Erika blew one of those paper horns at her. Meg stopped spinning, biting and piddling immediately, then ran straight for her bed to lie down quietly. Erika said it was as if in all the excitement, Meg realized she was out of control and came back to her senses. "Oh, yes, I'm bad. I'll just go lie down for awhile. Sorry." This is much better than any shock collar or professional canine counseling. I have several of these what I now call "correctors" around the house, on the patio and in the car. If Meg becomes too relentless with ball fetching, tail chasing, jumping, biting—I just reach for the "corrector" and point it at her. I don't even have to raise it to my lips and blow-Meg immediately runs for the nearest bed and lies down. Once I caught her trying to run off with one of the "correctors" in her mouth, but I caught her in time and rescued this amazing eliminator of bad behavior.

Meg also chases the beams of both headlights and flashlights. I have shined flashlights around dark rooms just to watch her dash after the beams; this also works with reflections of light off of mirrors and watch faces. When she was still a puppy, she would try to jump into the bathtub with me in order to bite the bubbles. The door now remains closed when I am relaxing in the tub.

There is a rather cool gizmo I purchased from a gardeners' catalog to deter deer from my landscaping. It's a black plastic contraption that screws into the ground with a garden hose attached to it, powered by a nine volt battery. It comes complete with black and orange stickers you can affix to it which are supposed to simulate eyes. A motion sensor detects any movement in a 25-30 foot radius, thus causing a long rapid fire spray of water to circulate that will discourage marauding fur bags (deer). Meg discovered this great invention, believing it was made for her personal entertainment. She rushes up to it, causing the water to spray forth, biting and growling at the strongly pulsing stream. She gets her mouth on top of it, actually snapping her teeth up and down on the spray that causes her to begin choking from all the water pounding down her throat! After 15 or 20 minutes of this intense hysteria on the part of the audience, the "Scarecrow" has to be shut off before the well runs dry, the battery runs down, or Meg practically drowns.

Erika and I discovered a discarded paperback entitled "How to Test Your Dog's IQ." We were both laughing so hard we could barely breathe, thinking about testing Meg. One of the tests involved showing your dog a couple of empty bowls and then letting the pet watch you hide a treat under one of the overturned bowls. Then you time your furry friend to see how long it takes the test subject to overturn the correct bowl and enjoy the treat. Meg never even tried; another dog staying with us did it in five seconds. Thirty seconds or less was good, indicating your dog was fairly bright. I thought about using a tennis ball instead and voila! Meg is a genius after all.

I like to watch TV programs with animals such as "Animal Planet" and "Evan Almighty," because Meg enjoys them as well. She runs over to the screen and puts her front paws on the cabinet so she can stand on her hind legs to get a better look, especially if there are dogs on the program. Sometimes I find movies with featured dogs who aren't always exhibiting proper dog behaviors, so I find myself thinking I should change the channel before Meg gets the wrong idea. Recently, Meg and I were watching a movie with a bionic dog that began taking revenge on people who were cruelly abusing the animal. I could honestly see the look on Meg's face; her eyes were very sad and I felt I should apologize to her for not turning the movie off sooner.

A few years ago, Meg stayed almost a month with my good friend, Audrey, while we were on a two week cruise in the Pacific followed by a week in Sydney, Australia. She and her "fella" Nathan enjoyed taking Meg on walks with their dog, Cleo, who was becoming less mobile. Audrey said Meg's presence inspired Cleo to take longer walks and the two dogs became good friends. Audrey quite liked having Meg around. I even overheard her tell my own dear dog that Meg was welcome to come live with her and Nathan anytime. Audrey told me she was pleasantly surprised at how quickly Meg understood the routine around her house and learned how to use the doggy door almost instantly.

Then she said, "There is something I need to tell you about Meg." She said it so seriously I began to wonder if she discovered Meg had some horrible physical problem or disease. When Audrey softly touched my arm and said, "I don't think Meg is very psychologically robust," I couldn't stop laughing at the absolute truth of that statement before turning to her and saying, "Who really is?"

Just last week, my friend Susan invited Meg and I to join her and her Rottweiler, Ruby, for a hike. We met up with them on a sparsely used dirt road, and I let Meg run along her merry way without her leash as usual. She began running back and forth in her usual radiuses to make sure I was still nearby as she splashed in streams or chased squirrels, thoroughly enjoying the opportunity to play. My friend kept her dog leashed the whole time, fearing Ruby might want to chase passing cars, walkers, or bicyclists. Meg came near Ruby a few times in her ditzy blonde fashion, which caused Ruby to snarl and bare her teeth.

A few days later, we all met up again in Mountain Lakes Park to enjoy another outing. I asked Susan if it was all right to unleash Meg and she assured me it was fine. I trust her judgment because she has worked with dogs and knows her animal well. When she began to unleash Ruby, I was somewhat wary. I thought maybe I should whisper in Meg's ear to tell her to run and jump into the water if Ruby started to tear her apart, since Ruby doesn't like swimming. I believed Meg would roll over on her back and splay her legs apart, exhibiting her usual submissive behavior, so I was pleasantly shocked when Meg bared her teeth, curling back her upper lip and snarling in a manner I had never witnessed! I had a totally new respect for my girl, while Susan was delighted that Meg had stood her ground, causing Ruby to seek shelter behind her "Mom." It seems dogs who are basically afraid or insecure will put on a show of bravado that I found very convincing, but back down if the animal they are threatening shows any confidence at all; go Meg!

Sometimes I trust Meg too completely and she will quickly remind me she is still, after all, a dog. I rose early on Thanksgiving to make a couple of pumpkin pies and some butternut squash soup to take to my friend's house for dinner. I ran upstairs to get a shower before we left, forgetting Meg was downstairs. Anthony called upstairs as I was getting dried off to ask me if the pies were supposed to look like that and I told him the aluminum foil I'd put around the crust left a few marks in the pies that is nothing unusual. He wasn't sure, so Erika went down to look at the pies while I finished dressing and began laughing while Anthony began verbally escorting Meg from the house. I had left the pies too close to the kitchen counter to cool; this was too irresistible for Meg who had eaten as much of both pies as she could reach. I came downstairs to behold the carnage and decided to cut both pies in half and put the untouched halves together to make one pie to take. Anthony was disgusted with the strange pie as Erika and I continued giggling as we half-heartedly scolded Meg for her sneaky pie attack.

Just this past week, the septic tank was pumped out and once again, I almost trusted Meg too completely. The fellow cleaning the tank told me dogs were certainly attracted to sewage, which was alarming in itself as I noticed Meg had found one of her cherished tennis balls to offer up to the newcomer. I tossed the ball a few times and eventually failed to notice as Meg came closer to the menacing hole, dropping the ball and then watching as it fell into the tank! She stood there sadly watching the hole as the ball was sucked up into the hose and on into the tank on the truck, hopefully never to be seen again. After the truck drove away, she tried to dig up the freshly tamped earth covering the hole in hopes of retrieving her ball. I took her into the garage and shut the door, not wanting any part of that scenario. I wasted no time in walking over toward the neighbor's tennis court to find an errant ball to replace the one now floating along the murky, odious surface inside the truck sloshing down the road to its next destination.

When Anthony is away, I can't get Meg to come inside after 6pm in the evening. She wants to stay out in the garage and wait for "Dad" to drive into his spot. It takes a few days before she realizes it's just me and that's all, but it's good to have her tireless thirst for play and hikes. Without my best friend, life would be lonely indeed.

Pam Pooley

Silent Things

Carbon

The newly planted trees around the house looked sadly taut when I pulled in our driveway after being away for a week this July, one of many weeks of 90 degree temperatures and no rain. You could see the young birches and weeping willows and the crabapples that we'd planted just a few months before grimacing from too much heat and too little moisture. The branches hung with shrunken or sparse leaves, the canopies aching rather than relaxed.

I could only think "global warming" though climate change does not simply manifest itself in warmer weather. I explained this to a British friend of mine last winter, who was awed by the unusual amount of snowfall in London that year. She wasn't sure about global warming. I told her there's been a trend in warmer temperatures ever since the Industrial Revolution when we upped our emissions of carbon dioxide, which we know is a heat-trapping gas. It seems ironic that we could get more snow, but warmer air holds more water vapor. With temperatures rising and more moisture in the atmosphere, storms can become more turbulent, causing greater rain and snowfall.

My arborist explained to me that the stomata in trees close when it's so hot and dry, and that's why our young trees could die. I needed a refresher in botany to understand this. I read a tree fact: As much as 80 gallons of water can evaporate through the leaves of a mature tree on a hot summer day. Trees defend themselves during prolonged drought by shutting down transpiration, which means closing their stomata, the pores on their leaves, to keep moisture in. It's the emergency mode of a plant to conserve water and prevent evaporation.

But when this happens, the plant also blocks the entry of CO_2 required for the business of photosynthesis, and therefore starves itself. I learned the process is called "carbon starvation." It's one reason why scientists believe that climate change poses a risk to the natural world. During the European heat wave of 2003, the hottest time since 1500, a study showed that plant growth across the continent dropped 30 percent because photosynthesis stopped. So this leads me to think, if carbon dioxide fills our air, coming from cars, coal plants and the like, and our trees are shutting down their job of carbon cleansing when it's hot, we are left with a double whammy of carbon dioxide. I could become very depressed if I kept studying the science. It's easy to take for granted the silent work trees are doing for us.

The heat was bothering the animals as well. Coyotes were out during the day, lingering around in the rural fields near my house. This was unusual. I was afraid to walk my dogs. They even knew that the mangy canine slinking around the pasture was not one to play with. We would turn back. News reports told of coyotes biting young children in the busy suburbs down county. Everyone was grimacing.

Oil

We heard about severe weather conditions around the world this summer, devastating droughts in Russia and monsoon rains in Pakistan. The Indus River there was forty times more bloated than it had ever been. A disheartening op-ed in the New York Times, *A Lifetime, Washed Away* was written by a Pakistani mango farmer who said that the floods have caused a catastrophic loss of property—sweeping away villages and crops and animals, leaving people alive, but with nothing. The United Nations reported that at least six million people need emergency assistance, food, shelter, medical care. This is devastating. How can I help?

Praying for the health of the earth is overwhelming to me. I can pray for individuals, but praying for our entire planet is hard to get my mind around. My trip away in July had been to an environmental conference, which no doubt sensitized me to the state of our livable earth. I got a good dose of facts and figures. The United States represents 4.5% of the world's population, and contributes 25% of the world's greenhouse gas emissions. A presenter from National Geographic showed photographs of changes on our earth's surface, evaporating water ways, glacial melt, populations suffering from food shortages, animal extinction. What hit me most was a photo of a typical American backyard filled with large plastic playthings—jungle gyms, swing sets, wading pools, plastic bikes and plastic toys—all made from oil, we were reminded.

On the plane home I read a book called *Love God Heal Earth* by an activist Episcopal priest named Sally Bingham, who was at the conference. In her collection, religious leaders of all denominations write about our sacred duty to protect the environment. These Christians, Muslims, Jews and Buddhists united to form Interfaith Power and Light, an organization that helps people consider how to lower our carbon footprints.

Tonight I pick basil from our garden. I tell my teenage daughters that we will save electricity by making pesto the old-fashioned way with a mortar and pestle. Luckily, I find in *Essentials of Classic Italian Cooking* that Marcella Hazan says it's the authentic way to make pesto anyway. While I snip the basil, I feel better mumbling prayers of thanks, thanks for the basil, thanks that my well hasn't dried up, thanks for these little things.

Seeds

We have a big vegetable garden, twenty-five by twenty-five feet. My husband and I made it fifteen years ago with the stamina of being in our thirties. Over time I have replaced space for vegetables with perennials and roses because we could not keep up with eating, giving away or canning the harvest. We don't plant just one tomato, we plant half a dozen because there's so many different kinds. We buy a lot of our seeds from Seed Savers Exchange, which is a bank of rare heirloom seeds, more than 25,000 endangered species. The tomatoes of yore have great names like Hillbilly Potato Loaf and Red Zebra. It amazes me what one tiny seed will become. Over the course of the summer bare ground gives way to huge specimens of cauliflower, kale, brussel sprouts, and broccoli plants, which have leaf matter like low-lying umbrella colonies. Our property was once a cattle farm so that the soil is supercharged with organic matter.

This summer we tried a Native American planting scheme called the three sisters. The Iroquois Indians believed corn, beans and squash were precious gifts from the Great Spirit, watched over by one of three sister spirits, called the Sustainer spirit. The idea of sustainability comes alive with this practice. The corn is a natural pole for our heart-shaped string bean vines to climb. One bean seed leads to a marvelous progeny of beans and more beans, little cliques of three to six, finger-length string beans dangle from the corn stalks by early August. They fix nitrogen on the roots of the corn, which is great for the fertility of the soil. The summer squash leaves are like large hand fans, helping to conserve soil moisture and crowd out weeds. One small seed creates a weekly load of zucchinis, they can grow to the size of my husband's leg if we are not vigilant. What's more is that the three sisters complement each other nutritionally—corn with the carbs, beans the protein, while squash is full of vitamins. When the plants die back, they feed the soil with nutrients. How this threesome orchestrates life together is the crux of sustainability, a word that we hear a lot these days. It has to do with the value each member throws into the mix, each has a role and function, and there is no wasted energy.

Sea

I think extreme weather is trying to tell us to wake up, it's one of the few things we simply can't control, but it makes us look at ourselves and how we treat the planet. Can we look at nature not as victims, but as partners? Pema Chödrön, an American Buddhist nun looks at things this way: She says to move toward difficulty, rather than backing away from it. This sounds counterintuitive. We are told from childhood that something is wrong with the world, with us, and with everything that comes along, that it's not perfect. The main point of the Buddhist teachings is to stop struggling against what's happening to us or in us, but to take on life as it is. That means the fulfillment of a seed or the outcome of a flood are really both the same, not good or bad in this view, they are our life's agendas.

It's easiest to lay blame and be a victim though. I know this first hand. Last week I drove my daughter and her friends to a ferry they were catching in Cape Cod. To break up the drive, I stayed over the night in a hotel by the sea. When I woke the next morning I was instantly angry to hear what sounded like engines whining in the distance. Jet skis I was certain, and so early, ruining my solitude. More oil I thought, shouldn't "they" ban jet skis? I set down to the beach with my coffee and local muffin. As I looked out at the inlet beyond the moored fishing boats in the aptly-named Pleasant Bay harbor, I scanned for the jet skiers, revving in chorus at disturbing high pitches. I walked a few more yards to the shore, the water was ideally translucent in that morning light. Nymphs and baby fish dashed about, the sea looked clean, inviting, icy-feeling to my feet, even in August, as my eyes searched the distant shoal to locate that droning sound. Then, suddenly, the surprise of recognition. My breath stopped short as I became aware that the disturbing noise was not coming from motors, but from thousands of shiny, brown bald-headed seals. Hundreds were gathered like worshippers in the low tide, masses dotting the shoreline. I knew that I should be relieved, sing hallelujah, for this was a benign habitat. The wonder of the moment was glorious, but distress set in. The seals sounded upset, beached wounded souls, crying in chorus that reverberated through my being. It was hard to relax and be grateful, or muse with humor about my own misunderstanding. It was hard to stay there. I told my daughter about this and she calmly told me that's the sound seals make. Did she learn that at the Central Park Zoo? I felt the need to do some research on seals. Weren't they crying for the earth's pain? Or was it mine? I thought I should pray for them and for ourselves.

Rosalind Rock

The Mystery Ride

What a wonderful surprise—a charming, Baroque 16th century building, a warm and inviting intimate lobby, high ceilings, sparkling, luxurious decor, and the precious antique wooden elevator with its old-fashioned brass gate—to be my home during my stay in Cracow. The hotel's location in the Old Town—two blocks from the main square - with its walk-able streets radiating out from the center, make it a solo traveler's dream.

I was in Cracow to meet up with a colleague from London for the purpose of visiting the Chemar Plant that manufactured industrial valves for which I had found a potential joint venture partner.

In the early '90's, Central Europe, seemed like a golden opportunity for Western business people who saw tremendous investment potential in industrial collaboration. While some of us were conflicted by recognizing that the transformation to capitalism would result in irreversible changes in culture and tradition, we chose to envision bringing in Western hotel chains, commercial partners and retailers as a means of improving the lives of the local populations.

Such an opportunity presented itself when I entered the delicatesy in the square opposite the historic Cloth Hall. There was a buzz of activity around all the counters oozing with aromas and ample selections of Polish delicacies—the Dean and Deluca of Cracow. I wondered whether it was a stand-alone shop or a chain and who was the owner. I inquired of a young woman in the shop and gave a reason for my interest—primarily, that my company arranged "joint ventures."

When the woman phoned the manager and conveyed those two words—music to the ears of emerging market entrepreneurs who quickly embraced capitalism and its rewards—he agreed to meet me in my hotel at 7:00pm that evening. He said he would be wearing a green suit and green shoes.

When I emerged from the elevator to meet who I thought would be some sort of leprechaun, I saw an elderly man stand up to greet me. He spoke not a word of English, and I not a word of Polish. He introduced himself as Jan Ziska and beckoned me to follow him. He led me to his car, which was parked two blocks away. I got in and he started driving. We drove past several local streets before getting on the highway. After 15 minutes of driving and listening to a repetitious American pop song—while I was not terrified, it passed through my mind that this was a little crazy. I had no idea where I was going and not a soul knew whom I was with or my destination.

Was I too trusting in my desire to be part of this pioneering market transformation? After ten more minutes, we exited the highway and drove to a parking lot, which seemed to be on the grounds of a university. Mr. Ziska took a package from the car and as I followed he entered a building and took the elevator to the 3rd floor. He rang the bell of an apartment and a woman with a young child next to her answered the door.

They were his daughter and granddaughter. His daughter taught at the university. He had taken me there because she spoke some English. We sat down at a table and she translated her father's business proposition. He was the manager of a food co-op that had several shops in Cracow. One of the stores had a building that was not occupied. He wanted to know if I could find a Western user for it.

At the end of the brief discussion, we raised our glasses and drank the cold, slithery vodka—which I must say never tasted as good or as comforting.

Pat Skinger

Woman of Influence

My sister Sylvy will never forgive me for replacing her as the baby in the family. For her, that was my original sin, for me, my misfortune; I had upended her world. Throughout my life, my relationship with her has been developed from a cautious and considered distance, both geographical and emotional.

Sylvy's reputation as a "tearaway" preceded and followed her from an early age. Fiercely independent and always assured of her rightness, she shied away from no challenge; through strong mindedness and at any cost, she overcame her obstacles. My father recalled how, at two years old when she tired of walking, she would stop in the street, sit down and not move until someone picked her up and carried her. Bribes and threats were met with screaming protests and vehement refusals to walk any further. This could be true of any two year old, but the intensity of her refusal to comply, was a hint of things to come. Both my mum and dad struggled with her and often gave up. I always thought this was because she was the favorite child. Perhaps that was true, but it may have been a case of saving the big battles and with Sylvy there were frequent battles of one sort or another with outraged teachers and neighbors.

As an older child, she was at the core of numerous street fights, with her beautiful platinum hair flying, her pretty mouth set with an unyielding determination to be the victor, as she wildly scratched, pummeled and pulled the hair of her usually older and bigger opponents. She thrived on conflict and confrontation, proudly boasting of her conquests. Like a prizefighter going for the title, she was quick and clever and unafraid. Other children either loved or feared her.

I had mixed feelings. I was dominated by her, never having the courage to stand up for myself, but I envied her strength and was in awe of her daring behavior.

At school she was the one the teachers punished but with no effect. The more they punished her, the more intensely she defied them. When I followed her in grade school, I was admonished by several teachers not to repeat Sylvy's behavior. They could have saved themselves the trouble. I had none of her spirit, none of her courage. I dutifully followed the rules, not daring to question any authority. How different we were. Sylvy questioned everything. She once questioned the disapproving attitude of a malicious needlework teacher noted for humiliating the children. Miss Gates was teaching Sylvy the basics of knitting. In a rebellious response to her cutting remarks, my sister threw the knitting at the teacher and ran out of the class with a slam of the door. She was never permitted back into that class, but ironically she became an expert knitter creating various beautiful items in an array of exotic and artistic designs. My response to that teacher was total submission. When Sylvy was eleven she was appointed by the school to be a prefect. This was a highly coveted position and a source of great pride to my mother and even greater surprise to the rest of the family. I think this was a strategy that the teachers felt would encourage Sylvy's sense of right behavior and team spirit. With any luck, it would channel her energies to more positive cooperation. A school prefect oversees the younger children especially while moving on the staircases. Any child pulled out of line for disorderly conduct must be sent to the headmistress. I was the first and only child my sister ever pulled out of line; I don't know why but she did stop short of sending me to the headmistress.

She was a demanding child and a demanding woman who got her way in most things and in most relationships. She made things happen, according to her will. People were reluctant to upset her as the results could be like a volcano erupting. With all his rigidity and harsh discipline, my father could not control her and they were always in combat, even at his deathbed.

I spent most of my childhood coming out of the wrong end of a physical battle with her. Most of these battles resulted partly from her destruction of my games (she loved to toss my cut out dolls all over the floor and punch my stuffed elephant) or from my telling tales on her. "Cry baby," she taunted.

At family parties, Sylvy was the star, always eager to get up and sing and dance producing vivid and spontaneous performances. She had a natural talent for the piano and played by ear, keeping guests of all ages entertained. Another of her talents was mimicking people. The precision with which she captured the essence of a person was amazing and a great source of amusement. She was especially adept at mimicking me and no feeling was spared as she exposed my entire physical and mental shortcoming to her audience, always emphasizing my most acute vulnerability: an overbite. In a highly focused manner, she stuck her teeth at least an inch over her lips as she launched into stories about her little sister with the rabbit's teeth. For most of my life, I avoided smiling so that my teeth were not being exposed.

She grew into an exceedingly pretty girl, which together with her vibrant personality, her wit and sense of fun, attracted many friends and admirers. Appearances were of the utmost importance to her and she married a man whose stunning good looks were intimidating. In defiance of my father, she married Reg when she was barely eighteen and he twenty. They were a striking looking, party loving couple, but both immature and self-centered. When their beautiful son was born, neither one of them was prepared to cope with the burdens of caring for a newborn. Stephen was left in the care of relatives while my sister continued to work. I adored him and loved to be with him but he was a fretful and restless child.

From early childhood, Sylvy was a brilliant organizer. Her possessions were immaculate and rarely damaged or mislaid. She regarded with contempt others, who were, in her opinion, careless in their appearance, perhaps sporting scuffed shoes, garish jewelry or poorly groomed hair. Nothing escaped her attention. It was and is still a standing joke in the family that a visit with Sylvy requires considerable expenditure of time and energy to prepare, so as to pass muster. I still panic if there is a spontaneous get together.

Her organizational skills were highly prized by her employers. She was the person who met any deadline, and introduced greater efficiencies into any project she was involved in. Highly imaginative she accomplished her goals in notable style. It was as if every job was of the utmost importance to her and she demanded perfection of herself and others.

Her young daughter at 10 years of age entered a fancy dress contest to commemorate the 25th anniversary of the coronation. Captivated by this challenge, my sister determined that Hayley would win the contest. She launched into the project with all energy, flair and determination to win, resulting in the creation of the winning costume. Nothing was left to chance. Hayley became Queen Boadicea. Among the hundreds of contestants, she won first prize for originality and beauty in design and presentation.

Sylvy had the knack of winning—was it a strong focus or a determination to outshine everyone? I was the child in the family who wanted to write, talked about it, and took courses without actually producing anything notable. Sylvy surprised us all when she wrote a prizewinning article for a local newspaper. It was her only attempt at writing. I thought deeply about this asking myself how Sylvy, whose difficulty with spelling and lack of interest in writing and reading, had managed something that I, with all my studying and talking about had never managed to do. I felt proud of her but somewhat diminished as a result of this.

When my mother developed Alzheimer's Sylvy gave up her job and took charge of our mother's care, thoroughly tending to every detail of the situation and watching like a hawk any outsider who was involved. Not satisfied with the first diagnosis, she consulted four additional physicians. My brother, my sister Maureen and to a lesser extent me (I lived too far away) were severely criticized by Sylvy for not being more aware of the signs of our mother's illness and for not showing any initiative in dealing with it. Her criticism shamed us all, and brought about the same feelings I had around her as a child—she made me feel helpless yet at the same time, I found her strength and courage inspiring. I just envied her ability, her independent thinking and her strong spirit.

My brother recently arranged a Christmas get together at his home. Although the event was in January, my brother still had his tree on display. It was to be a festive dinner with my brother, his wife Eileen, my sister Maureen and her husband, Sylvy, by now divorced, and me, on a trip to England without my husband. My brother, my sisters and I had not celebrated a Christmas together since our own childhood.

Sitting around the roaring fire, we sent thoughts of love to our mother who had died a year earlier. Memories of childhood Christmases were recalled by all of us as presents were exchanged. Sylvy told me to read the message attached to her gift to me before opening it. Written on a card depicting a Dickensian Christmas scene was a note. She had written "When you were a little girl, more than anything you wanted one of those beautiful porcelain dolls that we saw in the store windows for Christmas, but mum could only afford a rag doll. The doll in the box is from me." I opened the box and there was Anastasia, exquisitely dressed in a ruby red velvet dress and matching bonnet. The outfit was completed with a matching parasol and black shiny boots.

I was deeply touched by Sylvy's thoughtfulness; even so as I leaned over to kiss her, I thought how predictable and unimaginative my gift to her was. Although I don't see Sylvy very much anymore (by her choice) she is still a big influence in how I view the world. She has, over the years, led me to look at myself and to see all my weakness and pretensions. She is cold in her appraisals and I say to myself "has she some special knowledge, some particular edge that the rest of us lack?" I want to love her but the demons in her put that love out of reach of either of us.

I recently told my brother that I was writing a story about Sylvy. "Is it a horror story?" he laughed. "Not entirely," I replied.

JANET WEIL

SPIRITS OF PETERSBURG

I am not religious, not in the conventional way, that is. I do believe the universe offers up mysterious signs to guide us. When I'm traveling, I try to stay attuned to those signs to direct me towards extraordinary locations and experiences that aren't listed in guidebooks. Perhaps, what I'm looking for when I travel is spiritual. I do not question whether the signs are cosmic or mere coincidence, whether the stars are in alignment or I'm in alignment with the universe and I have never regretted following their direction.

Mesmerized by the hundreds of bald eagles perched on old pilings jutting out of the sand along the beach, the ferry approaches our third stop on Alaska's Inside Passage-Petersburg. This bustling quaint fishing village is nestled along one of the most scenic sections of the Inside Passage, the protected waters of Wrangell Narrows, a twenty-two mile channel that is only three hundred feet wide in places. The twists and turns the ferry had to make through the channel were just short of a miracle. There were times I could almost touch the trees along the water's edge. As we approach the dock, dilapidated buildings in various stages of decay dot the shoreline. I hang over the railing watching as the ferry workers throw out the heavy ropes to the brawny muscled men on the dock, who then deftly twist and knot them around the pilings, safely securing the boat to the pier. As the ramp is lowered, Stan and I scurry down the stairway to our camper van parked below deck. Disembarking into the parking lot, we drive one short block to the center of this heavily Norwegian-influenced town, get out and wander the streets.

Strolling down to the busy dock, I glance across Frederick Sound at the spectacular glaciated wall of alpine peaks that form a skyline of jagged snowcapped summits. This dramatic landscape is not an unusual sight in Southeast Alaska, which is basically a five hundred mile-long strip of coastal islands connecting British Columbia to mainland Alaska. These islands form a protected waterway known as the Inside Passage. The region stands apart from the rest of Alaska for many reasons, surely the most influential one is that it cannot be reached by roads. Roads are simply too expensive to build through the icy mountains and across the jumbled terrain of islands. The steep glacial mountains lining the coast look like a gigantic hand pushed them forward and upwards while islands were stretched and scattered in the process. People are forced to slow down and travel by boat. Fortunately, the Alaskan Marine Highway, a system of inexpensive ferries connects the charming small towns and villages of these islands to each other and to mainland Alaska.

No other place in Alaska shares the mysterious, spirit-laden quality of the fabled Inside Passage, one of the rainiest places on earth. Tlingit and Haida natives have lived in this coastal rainforest for thousands of years fishing and hunting, building houses and totems, trading with faraway tribes and celebrating with potlatches. They believe there are spirits in every living animal, every being, that even the ice has a spirit. It is these native people who through their art, their dance, their stories and their totems that keep the spirits vibrant, pulsating, breathing.

Casually walking the network of docks out to the cannery buildings that still stand on long wooden piers, Stan stops and turns to me, "You know Janet, it's getting late. Let's find a campsite."

We drive out the road after nixing a campsite in town. A few miles further on, we stop at a small wooded campground with a friendly host couple, Rich and Kathy. They also own a general store well-stocked with booze—a big money-maker in these remote towns. After getting the van hooked up to the electrical and water connections and somewhat settled into our campsite, we mosey over to the store. Rich and Kathy are sitting on the front porch drinking wine and invite us to join them. I'm guessing they're in their early fifties. Rich is rather stocky but powerfully built with a head full of thick, blonde hair—a lively character with a permanent devilish grin, like he just heard a joke that no one else was privy to. Kathy has a straight-forward, no nonsense manner but she also seems fun-spirited. I peek through the open door of the laundry room and notice a clothesline decorating the back wall with perky clothespins clasping infant's clothing like treasured works of art. With rugged good looks, she reminds me of a model in an L.L Bean catalogue. We end up laughing and swapping stories well into the night.

"We moved to Petersburg right after we got married in 1978," Rich tells us as we sit down. "I was a civil engineer and got a government job building roads, supervising a crew. The land here, the land we built on was mostly muskeg. You know what muskeg is, don't ya? That spongy stuff that if you step on it, you sink down fifty feet. A real challenge for building roads, but we did it. I'll tell you something, lots of hard work went into building these roads. Built the road you drove out here on."

"Yeah, I sure as hell know what muskeg is," Stan smiles. "We played golf at Muskeg Meadows in Wrangell a few days ago. My ball went into the rough and I just left it there. A ball, even a good Titliest wasn't worth getting stuck in that spongy quicksand."

"I don't play golf but I've heard lots of stories about that course." Rich shakes his head chuckling.

"That's one golf course I'll never forget. I love their slogan, 'You've got to have a lot of balls to play Muskeg Meadows.' They got that right," Stan laughs.

"Nothing much here back in the seventies, just the town and it was pretty darn small," Kathy chimes in. "That's where we lived when we first got here—in town. Luckily there was a ferry then, too. We used it back then just like we do today—to go to Juneau if we want to shop or see a doctor. In fact, I'm going to Juneau tomorrow to see my dentist. Of course, I'll have to stay overnight at my friend's house. It's an eight hour boat trip."

"You have to travel eight hours on a ferry to go to the dentist?" I ask wide-eyed sitting straight up in my chair. "I drive ten minutes and I can be at any one of a dozen dentists. And I live in what's considered the *country*."

"I guess it's a trade-off. Actually, I love the ferry ride. The scenery is so incredibly beautiful. I never get tired of the views. All you have to do is sit there on the upper deck and watch one of the greatest shows on earth pass right in front of your eyes. Better than going to the movies, that's for sure. Of course you know that, you've been on the ferry. Betcha never see whales on the way to your dentist."

"No, no whales, just deer, they're all over the place. I love to look at them but they eat everything in sight. Hungry little buggers," I answer twisting my long curly hair around an elastic band.

Yawning, I turn to Stan and he nods at my unspoken signal. We're so connected after all these years together, we no longer need words to communicate. Just a look, a furrowed brow, a squeeze of the hand, a nudge, a nod, a tap on the foot and we each know exactly what the other is thinking.

"It was great talking with you guys. See you tomorrow," we smile and head back to our camper.

Early next morning while strolling around the campground drinking our coffee, Rich suggests a day trip for us—a drive out on an old logging road for an unparalleled view of glaciers and the surrounding mountains.

"There's nothing like it. The views are spectacular!" he claims. "The road is rough going at times, but I'm sure your van can make it."

"We trust you Rich. You've been around these parts for a long time. You wouldn't lead us anyplace we couldn't handle, now would you?" I good-naturedly ask.

"You're gonna love it. I'm telling you, it's worth giving it a try," he reassures us.

Stan looks at me and shrugs, "Sounds like a plan. Let's do it." I agree and he unhooks the camper and off we go.

Glancing at the date on my cell phone, I realize today is July 17th my sister Susie's birthday. Memories of her birth suddenly burst into my mind like fireworks on the fourth of July. I was twelve-years-old the day my sister was born. Where to go biking, what tree to climb or when the ice cream truck would be in the neighborhood were my biggest concerns. When I awoke that hot summer morning, my father was downstairs in the family room nervously pacing the floor with my Aunt Annette, my mother's sister who lived right next door. They told me Mom was in the hospital. She had been in labor all night and there were complications. Dad had come home to be there when my older sister Barbara and I awoke so we wouldn't be frightened. Auntie was sobbing. Tearfully, she implored me to pray for my mother. I was confused by Auntie's weeping and terrified something was wrong with my mother. Racing upstairs to my bedroom, I got down on my knees and recited the rosary to the Blessed Virgin Mary over and over again. My father went back to the hospital and after what seemed like an eternity, he came home to tell me my mother was fine and I had a new baby sister. I was so relieved and excited, I went running out to the street and over to my friend Madge's house shouting out the good news, "I have a new baby sister! I have a new baby sister!" to everyone I met.

Susan and I were deeply connected. I was the big sister to whom she turned for advice and looked up to as a role model. Susie brought laughter to our serious family. She was always playing the clown, imitating commercials at dinnertime or with her silly antics tried to get a laugh anyway she could. Nothing ruffled her feathers. Once after babysitting for me, when I was taking her home, she walked out to the car barefoot. I asked her where her shoes were and she just shrugged and said, "I left my shoes by the front door and Dylan [our dog] peed in my shoe, so I threw them out. I didn't like those shoes much anyway," she laughed. We both loved to paint and did all sorts of crafty projects together- like the time we painted my mailbox with butterflies and flowers or the kid's bedroom ceiling with cotton candy clouds.

One Christmas, I took her to the Roosevelt Field mall to buy a dress for her holiday gift. Before shopping, we went to a café for lunch. I wanted to savor this time alone with Susie. One on one time didn't happen very much anymore. Now that she was a teenager with lots of friends and I was married with two kids, we spent less time together, just the two of us. Laughing and chatting excitedly about the guy she was going to the Junior Prom with, we headed into Macy's. I watched her rifle through the clothes racks and saw her pause at a beautiful green velvet dress, smile, look at the price tag and then continue searching.

With her arms full of dresses ready to go into the fitting room, I looked at her puzzled asking, "Why don't you try on that green velvet dress you like so much?"

"Oh, that's too expensive," she mumbled shaking her head.

"Go on Susan, try it on. It's fine, really. If you like it, you can have it. I want to get you something special, something you really want," I pleaded with her grabbing the dress off the rack.

She finally agreed to try it on and instantly fell in love with it. When she walked out of the dressing room blonde hair swinging on her shoulders, long legs striding towards the mirror, innocence transforming, I had to smile. Such dazzling beauty!

Jarred out of my reverie after almost an hour of switch-backing up the bumpy potholed road, I have an amazing insight. This abandoned logging road is not only incredibly steep, it's dangerously narrow. We're deep in the forest and have not seen a single soul, not one car, not a truck, nothing since starting up.

"Stan, are we insane? If we get stuck out here on this deserted road, we're dead. We have no cell service and it's at least a twenty-five mile walk back through this mountain to the main road," I blurt out feeling very edgy.

"It's too steep, too narrow. How do we know which turn-off to take? It could be any one of these," I nervously continue jumping around in my seat.

"Take it easy, Janet. I have no idea which way to go. I'll turn around at the next pull-off, head back and we'll just forget this whole idea," Stan flashes back.

"Maybe, we should do just that! I know how you hate to turn back, no matter what," I snap at him thinking, *he's not turning around. He never turns around.*

We drive around a bend and suddenly there's a red jeep coming right at us. It stops and so do we. A solidly built, dark-haired guy leaps out and strolls over to our van with a cool, not-in-any-big-hurry kind of walk. He has a big grin on his face and greets us with a friendly, "Hi there folks, where you going?"

We tell him we're headed to the top of the mountain for the views and he reassures us that the road doesn't get any worse. Encouragingly he adds, "The view from the summit is well worth driving up this steep, rutted road. I'm sure you can do it and there's enough room to easily turn around once you do get up there. C'mon, follow me."

"Hey thanks, but you don't need to go out of your way for us," Stan assures him leaning out the window.

"No, no, it's fine—really, I insist. C'mon let's go." Hopping back into his jeep, he backs up, turns around and zooms up the mountain road.

We try to follow close behind but lose him momentarily at a fork in the road. "Turn right and keep going up," I direct Stan listening to my instincts.

Sure enough, this guy is a little ways up waiting for 'the adventurous souls from New York,' as he has now dubbed us. Climbing slowly but steadily up the rocky road, we lose him several more times but he waits each time for us to catch up, smiling and waving us on. Finally, after more than an hour, we reach the summit. I jump out and spin around gasping at the uninterrupted view of at least a hundred miles in every direction.

"Look Mom, I'm on top of the world!" I playfully shout, arms held high.

I learn this kind stranger's name is Ted but he skillfully deflects any other questions about himself other then to say he has been in these parts for many years. He points to the jagged snowy mountain peaks across the sound and to Le Conte glacier and the broken ice floes at its feet. Scanning the landscape, the breathtaking beauty of the Narrows and straights of the Inside Passage slowly unfold before our eyes. The cobalt blue water snakes through the sheer vertical peaks ever pointing towards the heavens with the frozen glacier yawning at its feet. The brilliantly clear crystal blue sky sparkles in unison.

But the warmth and caring of this stranger is as remarkable as any view. Actually, I find it quite extraordinary. Ted had no reason to interrupt his day and take so much of his time to patiently help us on our journey up the mountain except for the generous nature of his heart. This gift of unsolicited generosity, I highly treasure. We expect kind acts from our family and friends but the unexpected kindness of a stranger always astonishes me. How curious that the kind acts of strangers seem to reverberate on and on, like a bubble at the bottom of a pond that eventually emerges on the surface and sends out ripples across the water. I always smile when I remember the kind gestures of strangers no matter how long ago it was.

There was an incident decades ago, when late one hot summer afternoon on the parkway driving home from the ocean with a car full of hungry and tired little boys, I got a flat tire. While looking bleakly at the punctured tire as four little rascals are jumping all over the car, a man stops on his way home after a long day of work, changes my tire and takes off before I could properly thank him. Or, the time a waitress in a restaurant in Brooklyn picked up my purse from the back of the chair after I had left the city and called me to let me know my credit cards, cell phone, two hundred dollars and a pair of prescription sunglasses were there waiting for me whenever I wanted to come get them. Or, or, or… I could easily go on but the truth is these simple kind acts of strangers are really quite extraordinary in their impact. They are what give me my trust back in humanity, the kind of trust that only small children and dogs have.

Ted asks if we want to get some semi-precious stones on the other side of the mountain.

"You can pick garnets right off the ground—big ones, too. I'll take you there," he offers.

I show him my garnet ring, Susie's ring. I've worn it ever since the police gave the ring to my mother after the fatal car accident that took her life.

"Thanks, but I have the only garnet I ever want. You've been a godsend Ted. We'll never forget you." I smile warmly and we all shake hands.

Jumping back into his jeep, he grins and waves to us. And like a puff of smoke he disappears down the mountain just as mysteriously as he appeared.

And just like a puff of smoke, my sister Susie disappeared one hot August night. She and my parents had come over to my house for a Labor Day barbecue. In a few days, Susie would enter her senior year of high school. She played *The Who's* album, "Tommy" so that she and her nephews could listen to it together before dinner. After finishing her blueberry pie and excitedly talking to her friend on the phone, she asked Dad and Mom if she could walk over to her friend Patty's house and then go to Garvies Point for an end of the summer beach party. They agreed. She kissed everyone good-bye and with what would be her last words to me, "Thanks Janet for everything. I love you," walked out my front door.

A few minutes later, my father suddenly jumped up from his chair and went running out to the street. Susie was at the crest of the hill and he called to her. She stopped and turned around just as the sun was setting casting a warm glow all around her while tinting the sky a brilliant orange. He asked if she wanted a ride.

She smiled and said, "No thanks, Dad. I'd like to walk there myself. Bye, see you later."

At 9:20 that evening, the time is etched forever in my mind, the phone rang. I answered it and a very controlled voice said, "This is Glen Cove Hospital. There's been a car accident. Susan Stanley is here in the emergency room. Come quickly, she's seriously injured."

Feeling like someone was holding my head underwater, I gasped for air and handed the phone to my father. The deadly message was repeated. Stan and Dad rushed to the hospital while I stayed at home with my sons and my mother who couldn't bring herself to go. She feared the worst and was not able to face it. Mom and I paced back and forth in the living room looking expectantly out the front window. We held our breath every time a car drove down the street. Waiting…Hoping…Praying… My boys, only eight and nine years old at the time stayed in their room confused and frightened. I periodically ran into their bedroom, grabbed them close to me hugging them tightly.

When Stan and Dad got to the hospital, the emergency room was swarming with Susie's friends who were at the scene of the accident, which was less than a half-a-mile from the beach party. Word had spread quickly. The doctor greeted Stan and Dad gently leading my father to a chair. Dazed and confused, he sat down.

Then, the doctor took Stan aside quietly telling him that Susan was gone. "She died in the ambulance… We did everything we could… I'm so sorry… The priest is on his way… Would you please come with me and identify her body for us?"

Stan never heard anything past, "she died…" He staggered behind the doctor as if cast into a hypnotic trance. He looked at Susie's beautiful face which miraculously had no cuts or bruises despite her being propelled into a telephone pole at sixty miles an hour. Tearfully, he nodded to the doctor. He later told me she looked like she was just sleeping. He stood there paralyzed, unable to move, staring at her expecting her to awaken at any moment.

The priest rushed into the emergency room, found my father and sat down next to him. How do you tell a father his beautiful, seventeen-year-old daughter is dead? Putting an arm around my father's shoulder, he simply said the unspeakable. He then went into the room where Susie was and anointed her body, blessing her journey. After the priest left, Stan and Dad mournfully came home. I heard the car in the driveway and raced to the front door flinging it open. They stood on the front porch huddled together sobbing and I immediately knew the truth.

Stan looked at me and blurted out, "Susie's dead!"

I doubled over with a piercing pain in my gut feeling as if someone had violently thrust a knife into me crying, "No... No... No..." I ran to the farthest corner of the house but there was no escape. "No, she can't be dead. It's not possible. She was just here eating dinner," I moaned in disbelief. "She's only seventeen—just seventeen. She has to graduate and go to art school and become a great artist and be my friend forever," I agonizingly lamented.

Our house became the gathering place for the family that night of darkness and pain. Mom, Dad, Barbara and I sat on my bed, weeping and embraced each other as a family. It was the most intimate moment I have ever experienced with them. Death was so sudden, so unexpected, so final!

The next day, tearfully staring at the clothes in her closet, I chose to bury her in the velvet dress she and I had bought at Christmas only eight months ago. At that moment, I felt as if Susie was choosing it, certain it was the dress she wanted to wear to her farewell ceremony. She was seventeen when she left us, a blossoming young girl, a flower slowly unfolding, one perfect petal at a time.

After three months of going through the motions of living like a battery-operated robot, one afternoon my friend Lisa said to me, "Janet, your boys need you to be their mother again. They miss you."

Feeling like a diver with a tank low on air who got distracted by all the sights underwater and forgot to come up to the surface, I slowly emerged from the darkness and rejoined the living. The constant pain in my heart, the daily crying jags lessened and eventually disappeared. The connection with Susie's spirit became stronger as time went on. I saw her smile in the woman at the check-out counter's smile, the sparkle in her big brown eyes in the twinkle of my son's teacher's eyes, the tilt of her head in a twist of a stranger's head offering me a hand, her loving reassurance in the dozens of lost articles I have found when I asked her for help. Susie's generous spirit lives in the kind acts of strangers, people like Ted, the man who changed my tire, the waitress in Brooklyn and countless others who have brightened my path.

Most clearly though, I see Susie's gentle beauty in my daughter Rebecca. Although Rebecca was born seven years after Susie died, she has always felt a powerful connection with my sister. At times, I feel like I am the link between the two of them. Or, are they linking me to them? It's as if they were best friends in another time, another place, another reality; soulmates of sorts. Rebecca's artistic creative talents and her extraordinary generous heart mirror Susan's. Rebecca's beauty is a brilliant reflection of Susie's—the smile, the sparkle, the whimsy, always believing the very best of everyone. One's goodness echoes the others. It's as if where Susie left off, Rebecca continues expanding.

It was Susan's death that helped define my spirituality. She connects me to the life force that beats through every being in this world and in worlds beyond. I have her in my life in a mysterious and powerful way. I am immensely grateful for all the love, the joy and the friendship she gave me when she was alive but equally grateful for the spiritual connection I have with her in the present day. Lucky me!

Gazing across the sound from my mountaintop perch, I hug Stan and whisper, "Happy Birthday, Susie and thank you for this gift."

Courtnea Whitehill

Tending the Turkeys

During my stay on the "foster home farm," one of my chores was to watch over the turkeys from the time they arrived in early spring until they were slaughtered just before Thanksgiving.

I never knew that it is so true how ignorant these creatures are!

The boys in the foster home would feed the birds in the early morning and let them (actually chase them) out of their hand-made wire cage and set them free for the day. Now they are called "free range," then they were called "loose turkeys!"

I hated to get the supper dishes finished and see the sun begin to set because that meant Bertha and I had one more chore before the end of the day. We had to go out into the fields and hills behind the barns and try to lure the screaming white birds, afraid of everything, not only us, would not stop gobbling and trying to get away from the two girls trying to chase them into their pen.

Then a break would come! One or two of them would follow us into the cage! We'd start spreading the food (pellets) and pour fresh water and soon, the rest would start coming in. Usually, it was well after dark before this chore was done, either officially or unofficially.

Officially, of course meant that we actually had taken an accurate count. I think we always had in the vicinity of one hundred each count. Unofficially, meant that we finally gave up, it was too dark, and no one really cared anyway. We closed the pen, and found our way back to the house, and went to bed ourselves.

We never ended up with one hundred turkeys at the end of the season. There was always a casualty or two, dogs, foxes, etc. We may have even beaten one or two a little too much with a stick trying to get them into that darned cage!

Night after night, they just never got it! Who knew?

I would never have anything to do with the slaughter, and I never ate turkey at that foster home.

After Bertha left, I was relieved of that chore since I couldn't and wouldn't do it alone, so in a way it was a gift Bertha gave me when she went away. I missed her so much.

POETRY

Claire Aldrich

Quiet This Storm

Quiet this storm
That rages inside me

Quell these flames
That smolder on

Spine to spine
Intertwined
My neck inclines
To reach that inner arc
Of your neck
Inclining towards me

We embrace
in a kiss
so long,
so deep,
so soft,
and so sensuous
there can be
no
other
kisss
in thiss
universse

12/28/96

Claire Aldrich

Wintersong

Go back
Go back
To when you first came
And you were whole

Go down
Go down
To Gaia's
Inner molten core
Fiery beauty
Reverberates
Through you
Cleansing you
Burning impurities
To ash

Rise up
Rise up
To a black star glowing
So many
Surrounding you
Beauty all around
Is you.

In these places
Of perfect beginning
In the miracle of
Form meeting spirit

You are whole
And perfect
And beautiful.

Dance!

Winter solstice
December 20, 1997
Moon in Virgo

Claire Aldrich

The Night Before I Met You

The night before I met you
I stepped out of the city
And set off homeward across the park.

Rolling along silently
Through the darkening, moist, eerie-quiet
expanse of night,
Ebbing din yielding to hushed soughing,
Fields melted into moors.

Dampish black branches
Reached out and around,
Scraping the sky
An old crone's craggy fingers
Sheathing fragile tendrils poised to shoot,
Ripe with promise.

And the moon
Hanging full
Shining bright in the soft grey night sky
Was all mine.

2/11/1998

CLAIRE ALDRICH

WHERE IS THAT PLACE

Where is that place
That I should go
Far from the minds of men?

Where sea shells spread in a tender garden
Full of cyclamen

And rose petals,
And marigolds,
Awild in lovely bloom,

With a softness in my eye
And a warmth in my heart
Ready to make room

For the one I know
Who will come to me
Some day when I least suspect

If I could only remember
To forget for a while
And stop learning to suspect.

May 1998
(on an inspired walk home along Park Avenue amid a wild breeze blowing)

Claire Aldrich

Venus

Venus like
A beauty mark
Freckles the moon,
Eye of the night sky

Lovely mole and moon
Alone on a stark field of midnight blue

Soft September evening breezes
give sound to
Rustling, drying leaves
Heralding the harvest
I know is coming

Standing by the black wrought iron gate
That gleams in the lamplight
Of a window where
Opera wafts faintly
My own soul begins to drift with the moon

Russian man and hounds approach.

Labor day weekend
Street corner, off an Upper West Side avenue
September, 1998

Christopher Bittner

The Meeting Ground

Standing at the edge in nutmeg sand,
The ocean desires to stand still, the beach.
Her feet sink in at the meeting ground,
She's not quite so sure which way to point them.

When she comes here it's to sort things out:
The tan and smell of island fish, the air brushing
Her nape at sunset, Bill's smile, the sound of
The children's play, remote, the lighthouse.

Again she can cry at waters edge.
Every year she has made it here,
Come once again as if to be spawning
Did we really come from the sea?

CHRISTOPHER BITTNER

BLUE MOUNTAINS

As the roar of the crowd dies down,
A golden blanket descends on blue mountains
And the purple valley murmurs.

Dusk brings with it silence,
In its own right, every day.
The sun must fall from the bloody sky.
One lives as long as possible.

What of the corral, the horses, the cowboys?
Their lives are paid for with a crimson ticket.
The matador has done his job and done it well
The supper bell rings. Dinner is on the table.

CHRISTOPHER BITTNER

DUST

Who is it that lies
On my table, my bookcase?
Tidy in the cupboard
My soup bowls hide away.

Kings and paupers both linger
In the living room-no favorites
Played here-no, we're not alone,
Though their tongues are now silent.

Monks with brooms remember their fate.
Acolytes wave urns of bitter incense.
Whole nations are swept away on Tuesday.
The maid doesn't know what she's doing.

Christopher Bittner

Little Words

Those little words of yours,
Winged off the tips of your fingers,
Render me silent.

Stilling the chatter swinging
To and fro inside my bird-cage mind,
I'm hiding away behind neatly woven wire
From those giant monsters peering in.

I peck at the gently scattered seeds
Of your assurances as the sun downs
And you wish me a kiss.

Your sweet sighs allay once again
My desire to flee with the door just ajar.
Bring me to rest on my pillow
With your little goodnights.

Christopher Bittner

Your Tears

Find your tears
Driving from work
In the middle of that song
The radio has saved
Just for you.

They will be there....
When you are ready to see,
They are caressing everything:
Snow flakes and raindrops
Like sunrays and ebb tides.

They fall on how hard this is,
From how much you try,
How everyone, on this highway
Like a flock of leaves, is driving home.

Barbara Livingston

For the Whaledreamers

Heal the earth
that we may heal ourselves
Cherish the wisdom which resides within each speck of dirt
each rock
each plant
each being – walking, crawling, gliding
Stories of the ages are within us
songs of creation binding us together
We came from her
We shall return to her

There is a voice in a vision
calling
Our mother cries out to us
looking for the antidote to the prolonged desecration
upon her soul
For she knows
and sends it to our dreams
Should we forget about her
we too shall be unremembered...

Peter Mullin

No Good-byes

And when I go—If "I" should go
And the dream of life is over
When wedding vows and time run out
Were my soul towards heaven sent.

Then do not be afraid my love,
And do not lie awake in sorrow
For I will not be gone for good
I will come back to you—perhaps tomorrow.

When St. Peter waiting at the gate
Would surely have to wonder
Though mortal eyes were opened wide
This one they'd not console
With a heart so broke and a soul so empty
Even heaven's glory couldn't hold.

And when at last we meet again
And soul to soul we're winging
Then the earth will hear no sweeter sound
Than the song of rescued lovers singing.

Peter Mullin

I Used To Be A Boy

I used to be a boy
And my little boy eyes
Saw straight
And my little boy hands
Picked out strong sticks
And smooth stones
To skip along the water
And my little boy feet
Led me into the woods.
Under shady summer canopies
I explored shallow caves,
I climbed all the good climbing trees
And I swung on the vines
That would hold my weight.
I turned over as many rocks as I could
To find toads and salamanders
Or an occasional snake.
I drank water from small streams
Like a dog on all fours
And never once got sick.
I sat on the tall flat rocks
In the sun
Listening to the birds
And the highway cars in the distance.
I would walk for hours
Alone and unhurried,
Looking up the trunks of tall straight trees
Into the sunlight.

I went into the woods empty handed
But I came out filled
Peaceful and content.
I used to be a boy
And my little boy eyes
Saw straight.

Peter Mullin

True Love

If you find someone (in this crazy world)
And you fall in love
And if you love them with everything that you are
And they love you in return
And day by day they come to know you and understand you
Your anger and your sadness
What stirs you and what stops you
And they still love you - only more so
If each day begins and ends with them
And the borders of your lives
Gets so mixed and re-measured and reborn
That you start making plans together
Sharing cherished dreams and secrets
Building a private sanctuary within each others hearts
If you have quiet walks and laughter
And Sunday Afternoons
If there is a bridge between you
And your two souls meet in the middle
And something inside you says YES!
Hold on for dear life
Go to extremes to preserve that love
Give this "one thing" your all
For there is nothing more precious or sacred
Or grows more beautiful with time than
True Love

Peter Mullin

Maybe It's Not About You

Maybe it's not about you
You and your plans and your goals and ideas
And that big map you have pictured in your dreams
That will become the story of your life.

What if you're not here to "become" something
What if you're not here for "you"?

Suppose that some of us are only messengers
Sent to earth to step in
And by words or actions
Heal another's "brokenness"
That alone being your purpose here.

To be a bridge or an anchor or a guardrail.
Or wings so that someone else may take flight.

You, perhaps never to know flight
But knowing the gift of flight
Where is the tear in that?

What a sacred mission
What a holy sacrifice

And now—

Suppose that all of us are messengers
And that the strength of the fabric of life
Is in the sharing between the strands.

That the spiritual life and the human existence
Gets enriched and illuminated by that inter-connection.

And that there is divine and worldly peacefulness
In that surrender.

Peter Mullin

Old Titicus

The winter sun is setting low
On Titicus tonight
Her westward end is full of fire
As the day gives up its fading light

The sky's ablaze in yellow and red
As the darkness cools the day
But the faithful heart is ever warmed
By nature's passion play

And soon her icy roof will melt
A birth of sorts come spring
And ours is but to wait and wonder
What wonders will its coming bring

But still the heart is restless
For summers yet to come it yearns
With all our hopes and dreams invested
When will we ever learn

While the master of this—"weather"
And the owner of these open skies
Has blessed us twice with heavens
Once for our soul and once for our eyes

So set you down beside her shores
When winter's sun is setting low
And be of faith and trust in seasons
We've nowhere else but home to go

Suzanne Rossel

The Suit

The suit sat enticingly in the window as we walked
to the back of the store,
back where the *real* bride dresses hung.

My mind hung with the suit as they slipped dresses over my head.
Instead of the bouffant-skirted, satin and sequined girl in the mirror,
I envisioned myself in that sleek, off-white suit,
the skirt classically straight, mid-calf
a sexy slit in the back
the jacket tailored, long—down to my hips
a silk blouse blending with the suit,
encircling my neck, pearls,
in my ears, pearls.

So clear, but, I didn't try on the suit.
I didn't ask.
I dared not oppose the unspoken demands
for the undemanding snow-white, floor-length bride's dress,
that reassuring virgin facade.
There was no brave suit for our wedding day.

So long ago…
And yet, as I stand reviewing the day, this day, nine years later
I am struck by the woman I see in the mirror.

This woman, in a straight, form-hugging suit,
straight skirt, slit up the back,
a fitted, hip-encircling jacket

a stylish, off-white blouse
pearl necklace
pearl earrings.

I am wearing a suit
So like that suit in the window
The one I was afraid to claim.
I wonder if I am more the woman I hoped to see
today, the day we asked for our divorce?

1993

Suzanne Rossel

The Edge of the Ocean

I stand in the eddying water,
the pads of my feet massaged by smooth, rounded stones
watching as you and your Dad skip flat rocks across the undulating
Atlantic surface
dipping, skimming up; dipping, skimming up; dipping, plunking down,
disappearing
three times, you've done better.

I feel ownership of this moment, this place
Even as a wave rushes round my stance
Shifting the sand below my feet.
The smooth rocks slip from beneath me
moving out
down
the long sand slide
creating small water falls as the ocean
rushes back on itself
taking so much
in and out.
I must adapt,
position myself on other rocks
left by a previous wave.

Maybe rocks you have pitched
or another boy and father.

Wishing to contain what cannot be held
discomforted by the constant flowing movement,

owning no details
occupying no moments
dispossessed.

2009

Suzanne Rossel

What if God said, be happy?

What if God said
Be happy?
What would you do then?
The words on the plaque startled me,
Cracking something open inside.

Shocked,
After 18 months, I saw
The unseen, unread, unrecognized.
The sign that had been there all along
The simple question
Thummed my brain, challenging my heart.

What if God said be happy?
Enthralled,
Breath halted,
Suddenly separated from my sticky, self-absorption
Glimpsing unexpected possibility,
Robust repast for my hungering.

What if God said be happy?
Exhale,
Moment passed,
Panic rallied, filling the space;
Appetite again uncertain in the face of this
Potential plentitude.
Supportive skepticism impugned,
Surely, God and happy circle in separate spheres?

Certainty closed the door,
God is suffering, piety, unanswered prayers,
Yes, that is my God.

But there, barely audible
Amidst the chattering din
A forgotten voice queried,
What if that isn't God
What if you misread the signs?

What if God said
Be happy?
What would I do then?

2010

Suzanne Rossel

The Subway

He stands on the first landing of the 86th Street Station
neither on the street
nor at the subway level.
Pants and underwear rimming, mid thigh
hands behind his back, jutting his pelvis forward
his pink penis hanging flaccidly down.
Above him Manhattan sidewalks steam with the crush of purposeful people.
Below him the careening rushing business bodies push through turnstiles,
sardining onto trains.
He stands on the mid-landing stage, presenting a silent drama to those of us
trying valiantly to "miss" the show.
His pull magnetic—the physical presentation unavoidable.

Who is he, why is he doing this?
Young man, old man
from his penis, young
circumcised—someone at birth cared to take some skin.
When did the caring stop?

A momentary glance reveals,
his face calm, defiant, enraged, perhaps a bit deranged
Was that a smile?
A ripple down my arm, fear.
He's made it hard to ignore him with his screaming, silent stance.
In all he didn't get, he has discomforting comfort with his
Nakedness.

1997

SUZANNE ROSSEL

FALL

Leaves squeeze brilliance out of their life,
dancing with abandon to the ground,
now a crackling, tufted carpet,
leaf shapes still discernible in countless shades of brown.
Winter snow and ice will transform, reconstituting death making soil for new life.
Waiting, samaras nestle in the fertile floor-cover,
little helicopters programmed to float, fly and ferret out receptive earth,
each potential for a glorious maple.

Trees showcase the promise of ongoing life,
from buds, to green leaves, to brilliant colored death and reproduction.
a comforting repetition at times
but I remain unconvinced by this,
discomforting, impersonal, persistent, predictability.

Do we follow the same circular path as the trees?
What color and splendor falls from our lives?
What fertility is created by our deaths?
Does this fecundity balance the losses?

I am doubtful.
For seeing the possibilities of your death,
how could I not grieve the loss of your tender, loving face
and the caring of your heart for the singular me?

At this time of the year as the leaves squeeze brilliance out of their life,
do they cry as they are falling?

2008

About the Writers

Fiction

Alice H. Boxer has had essays published in the collection *Cheaper than Therapy* and Rosebud Magazine, where she was a runner-up in the Fifth Biennial X. J. Kennedy Award for non-fiction. "Traveler" is her first published short story.

Diana Barnard Richter is a former newspaper editor whose writing career goes back to fashion copy for a San Antonio store and blurbs extolling the virtues of Hollywood celebrities while she was an editor on the staff of Modern Screen magazine. She took a long maternity leave to raise four children before becoming arts/social editor, then managing editor of a weekly Connecticut newspaper. She now writes short stories, for fun and possibly profit.

Non-Fiction

Jean Goldsmith was born in Brooklyn before it was hip or chic, and grew up in Athens, Georgia where she wrote a feature column for the Athens Banner Herald before graduating to college columnist for the Atlanta Constitution at the University of Georgia. She moved to NYC and spent over twenty years as an advertising art director. Her comedy of manners was presented at the Ridgefield Theatre Barn. She is currently working on a novel.

Katherine Harris is a contemporary painter and printmaker, who has exhibited her art at regional museums and galleries in Massachusetts, Connecticut, Rhode Island and New York. She received her BFA, summa cum laude, from the University of Connecticut. This is her first publication.

Desta Lakew was born in Addis Ababa, Ethiopia where she grew up and spent her adolescent years during the Ethiopian Revolution of 1974. She moved to the United States in 1982 to attend college in New York.

Brenda Maddaluna grew up on a farm in Indiana, attended Indiana State University, moved to Puerto Rico, New York and now resides in South Carolina. A great deal of her writing has revolved around letters to her father who suffers from Alzheimer's disease. He keeps the letters and rereads them frequently to help him keep abreast of various family members and events.

Pam Pooley has lived with her family and Labrador Retrievers in Manhattan, London and North Salem. She enjoys nature, gardening, photography and writing.

Rosalind Rock has an international consulting firm that arranges joint ventures and raises capital, primarily, for Chinese and Indian companies as well as domestic start-ups. She has a Masters Degree in Education and an MBA in Finance and International Business from NYU Stern's Business School.

Pat Skinger lives in Goldens Bridge with her husband, guitarist Jim Skinger and Laddie, their cherished dog.

Janet Weil resides part time in South Salem, New York and in Crested Butte, Colorado with her husband Stan. She has three adult children. *Spirits of Petersburg* is an excerpt from her travel memoir, *I Dream of Alaska,* which she is currently working on about her four month camping odyssey into Alaska.

Courtnea Whitehill has lived in North Salem since 1973. She is married and has two children. Courtnea's favorite pastimes are writing, reading, gardening and caring for her pets.

POETRY

Claire Aldrich works in the financial world by day. She loves living in the country, and has nourished her love of poetry and creative writing over many years.

Christopher Bittner is a poet, musician, composer and rock sculptor residing in North Salem, N.Y. He makes no bones about hoarding stones and shells on Martha's Vineyard when he is there with his dogs.

Barbara Livingston is originally from San Francisco, CA. She has been writing poetry since high school with long breaks during the years her children were growing. She has two daughters and a grandson and a granddaughter.

Peter Mullin has worked as a carpenter for thirty years in northern Westchester. His passion in poetry is to talk about that inner journey that we're all on. The common thread that runs between tears of joy and tears of sadness.

Suzanne Eve Rossel is an ardent walker, finding much to inspire her during these times out of doors. She has always wanted to write and appreciates the opportunity to share her work with other North Salem writers.

Supporters

THE FOLLOWING PEOPLE ALSO HELPED FUND THIS FIRST ISSUE:

Claire Aldrich
Helen and Nicos Anthony
Chris and Peter Bliss
Alice and Harold Boxer
Gerald Campbell
Peg Clark and John O'Meara
The de Vaulx Family
Sarah Githens and Bob Keyser
The Gracie Family
Mr. and Mrs. Daniel Greene
Lois and Ken Lippmann
Frances Ott
Ellen and Tim Purdy
Carolyn and Allan Reznick
Edris and J.R. Scherer
Amy and Anthony Serra
Cathleen and Jerry Sulli

The Friends of the Ruth Keeler Memorial Library

You and your membership are important.

The diverse programs, from children's fun events to adult enrichment, are made possible through your volunteer help and membership support.

Please share your ideas for activities; we are always open to suggestions for the future.

Executive Board
President: Pat Malanchuk
Vice-President: Sally Morin
Secretary: Mary Ann Barbieri
Treasurer: Beatrice Kruchkow

"Don't tell me the moon is shining; show me the glint of light on broken glass" – Anton Chekhov

Congratulations to all!!

Patricia Grodd and Michael Stone

ELIZABETH and RICHARD O'LEARY

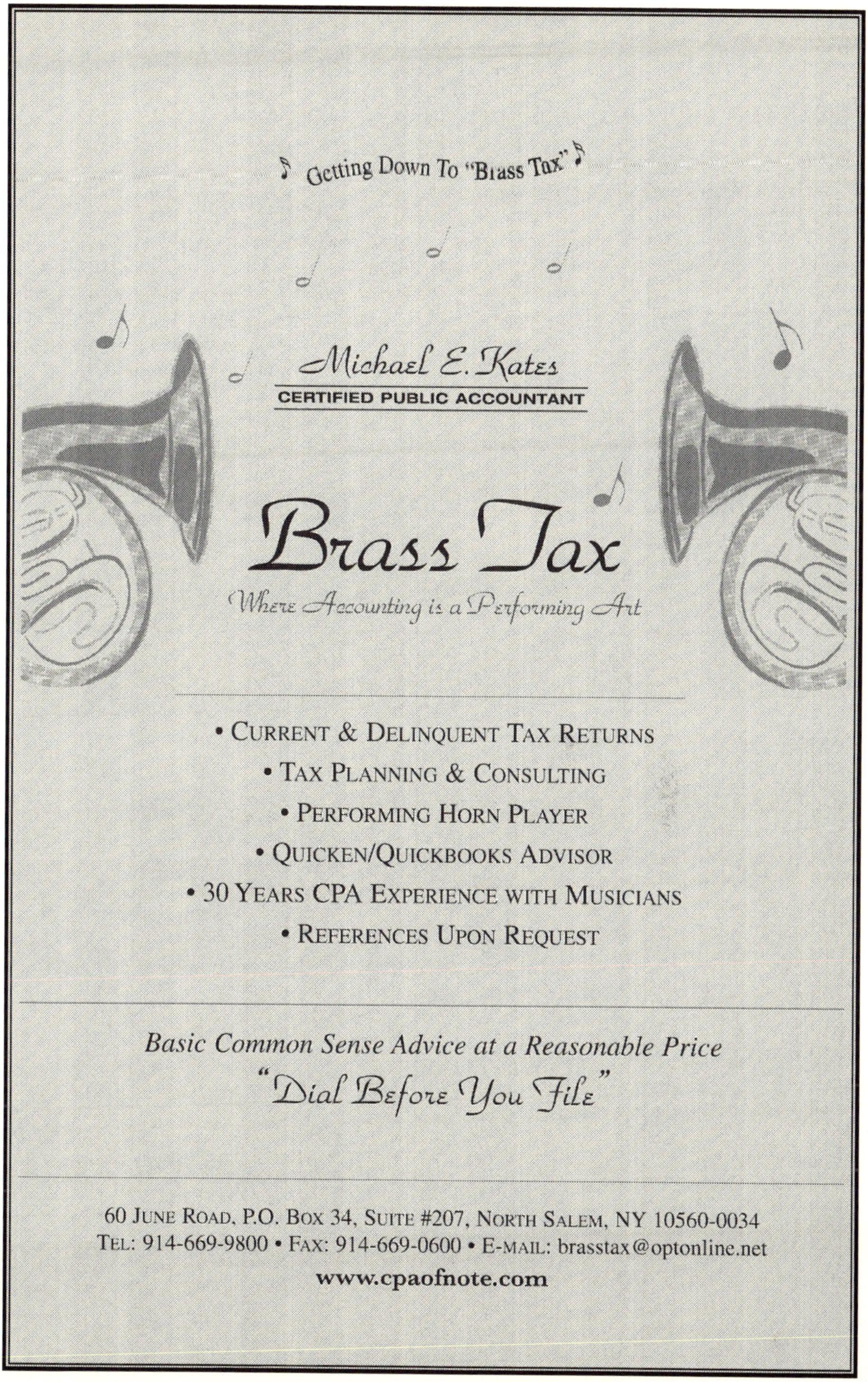
Getting Down To "Brass Tax"
Michael E. Kates
CERTIFIED PUBLIC ACCOUNTANT
Brass Tax
Where Accounting is a Performing Art
• CURRENT & DELINQUENT TAX RETURNS
• TAX PLANNING & CONSULTING
• PERFORMING HORN PLAYER
• QUICKEN/QUICKBOOKS ADVISOR
• 30 YEARS CPA EXPERIENCE WITH MUSICIANS
• REFERENCES UPON REQUEST
Basic Common Sense Advice at a Reasonable Price
"Dial Before You File"
60 JUNE ROAD, P.O. BOX 34, SUITE #207, NORTH SALEM, NY 10560-0034
TEL: 914-669-9800 • FAX: 914-669-0600 • E-MAIL: brasstax@optonline.net
www.cpaofnote.com

In loving memory of Ruth Keeler
who would have been so proud of the library
and this publication.

7647421R0

Made in the USA
Charleston, SC
27 March 2011